The Disappearance of Rituals

Byung-Chul Han

The Disappearance of Rituals
A Topology of the Present

Translated by Daniel Steuer

polity

Copyright © Byung-Chul Han 2020

First published in German as *Vom Verschwinden der Rituale* by Ullstein Buchverlage GmbH 2019

This English edition © 2020 by Polity Press

Polity Press
65 Bridge Street
Cambridge CB2 1UR, UK

Polity Press
101 Station Landing
Suite 300
Medford, MA 02155, USA

ISBN-13: 978-1-5095-4275-8
ISBN-13: 978-1-5095-4276-5 (paperback)

A catalogue record for this book is available from the British Library.

Typeset in 11.5 on 15 pt Janson Text by
Servis Filmsetting Limited, Stockport, Cheshire
Printed and bound in Great Britain by CPI Group (UK) Ltd, Croydon

The publisher has used its best endeavours to ensure that the URLs for external websites referred to in this book are correct and active at the time of going to press. However, the publisher has no responsibility for the websites and can make no guarantee that a site will remain live or that the content is or will remain appropriate.

Every effort has been made to trace all copyright holders, but if any have been overlooked the publisher will be pleased to include any necessary credits in any subsequent reprint or edition.

For further information on Polity, visit our website:
politybooks.com

CONTENTS

v

Preliminary Remark

The present essay is not animated by a desire to return to ritual. Rather, rituals serve as a background against which our present times may be seen to stand out more clearly. Avoiding nostalgia, I sketch a genealogy of their disappearance, a disappearance which, however, I do not interpret as an emancipatory process. Along the way, the pathologies of the present day will become visible, most of all the erosion of community. At the same time, I offer reflections on different forms of life that might be able to free our society from its collective narcissism.

1

The Compulsion of Production

Rituals are symbolic acts. They represent, and pass on, the values and orders on which a community is based. They bring forth a *community without communication*; today, however, *communication without community* prevails. Rituals are constituted by *symbolic perception*. Symbol (Greek: *symbolon*) originally referred to the sign of recognition between guest-friends (*tessera hospitalis*). One guest-friend broke a clay tablet in two, kept one half for himself and gave the other half to another as a sign of guest-friendship. Thus, a symbol serves the purpose of recognition. This recognition is a particular form of repetition:

> But what is recognition? It is surely not merely a question of seeing something for the second time. Nor does it imply a whole series of encounters. Recognition

1

means knowing something as that with which we are already acquainted. The unique process by which man 'makes himself at home in the world', to use a Hegelian phrase, is constituted by the fact that every act of recognition of something has already been liberated from our first contingent apprehension of it and is then raised into ideality. This is something that we are all familiar with. Recognition always implies that we have come to know something more authentically than we were able to do when caught up in our first encounter with it. Recognition elicits the permanent from the transient.[1]

Symbolic perception, as recognition, is a perception of the permanent: the world is shorn of its contingency and acquires durability. Today, the world is symbol-poor. Data and information do not possess symbolic force and so do not allow for recognition. Those images and metaphors which found meaning and community, and stabilize life, are lost in symbolic emptiness. The experience of duration diminishes, and contingency dramatically proliferates.

We can define rituals as *symbolic techniques of making oneself at home in the world*. They transform being-in-the-world into a *being-at-home*. They turn the world into a reliable place. They are to time what a home is to space: they render time *habitable*. They even make it *accessible*, like a house. They structure time, furnish it. In his novel *Citadelle*, Antoine de Saint-Exupéry describes rituals as *temporal techniques of making oneself at home in the world*:

And our immemorial rites are in Time what the dwelling is in Space. For it is well that the years should not seem to wear us away and disperse us like a handful of sand; rather they should fulfill us. It is meet that Time should be a building-up. Thus I go from one feast day to another, from anniversary to anniversary, from harvestide to harvestide as, when a child, I made my way from the Hall of Council to the rest room within my father's palace, where every footstep had a meaning.[2]

Today, time lacks a solid structure. It is not a house but an erratic stream. It disintegrates into a mere sequence of point-like presences; it rushes off. There is nothing to provide time with any *hold* [Halt]. Time that rushes off is not *habitable*.

Rituals stabilize life. To paraphrase Antoine Saint-Exupéry, we may say: *rituals are in life what things are in space*. For Hannah Arendt it is the *durability of things* that gives them their 'relative independence from men'. They 'have the function of stabilizing human life'. Their 'objectivity lies in the fact that . . . men, their ever-changing nature notwithstanding, can retrieve their sameness, that is, their identity, by being related to the same chair and the same table'.[3] In life, things serve as stabilizing resting points. Rituals serve the same purpose. Through their *self-sameness*, their *repetitiveness*, they stabilize life. They make life *last* [haltbar]. The contemporary compulsion to produce robs things of their endurance [Haltbarkeit]: it intentionally erodes duration in order to increase production, to force more consumption. *Lingering*, however, presupposes things that *endure*. If things are merely used up and consumed, there can be no lingering. And the same compulsion of production destabilizes life by undermining what is *enduring in life*. Thus, despite the fact that life expectancy is increasing, production is destroying *life's endurance*.

A smartphone is not a 'thing' in Arendt's sense. It lacks the very self-sameness that stabilizes life. It is also not a particularly enduring object. It differs from a thing like a table, which confronts me in its self-sameness. The content displayed on a smartphone, which demands our constant attention, is anything but self-same; the quick succession of bits of content displayed on a smartphone makes any *lingering* impossible. The restlessness inherent in the apparatus makes it a non-thing. The way in which people reach for their smartphones is also compulsive. But things should not compel us in this way.

Forms of ritual, such as manners, make possible both beautiful behaviour among humans and a beautiful, gentle treatment of things. In a ritual context, things are not consumed or used up [verbraucht] but *used* [gebraucht]. Thus, they can also become *old*. Under the compulsion of production, by contrast, we behave towards things, even towards the world, as consumers rather than as users. In return, they *consume us*. Relentless consumption surrounds us with disappearance, thus destabilizing life. Ritual practices ensure that we treat not only other people but also things in beautiful ways, that there is an affinity between us and other people as well as things:

> Mass teaches the priests to handle things in beautiful ways: the gentle holding of the chalice and the Host, the slow cleaning of the receptacles, the turning of the book's pages. And the result of the beautiful handling of things: a spirit-lifting gaiety.[4]

Today, we consume not only things themselves but also the emotions that are bound up with things. You cannot consume things endlessly, but emotions you can. Thus, emotions open up a new field of infinite consumption. The emotionalization of commodities and the associated aestheticization of commodities are subject to the compulsion of production. Their function is to increase consumption and production. As a consequence, the aesthetic is colonized by the economic.

Emotions are more fleeting than things; they therefore do not stabilize life. In consuming emotions we do not relate to things but to ourselves. What we seek is emotional authenticity. Thus, the consumption of emotions strengthens the narcissistic relationship to ourselves. The *relationship to the world* that we have by way of the mediation of things is thereby increasingly lost.

Values today also serve as things for individual consumption. They become commodities. Values such as justice, humanity or sustainability are exploited for profit. One fair-trade enterprise has the slogan: 'Change the world while drinking tea.'[5] Changing the world through consumption – that would be the end of the revolution. Nowadays one can purchase vegan shoes or clothes; soon there will probably be vegan smartphones too. Neoliberalism often makes use of morality for its own ends. Moral values are consumed as marks of distinction. They are credited to the ego-account, appreciating the value of self. They increase our narcissistic self-respect. Through values we relate not to community but to our own egos.

The symbol, the *tessera hospitalis*, seals the alliance between the guest-friends. The word *symbolon* is situated within the semantic horizon of relation, wholeness and salvation. According to the myth related by Aristophanes in Plato's *Symposium*, humans were originally globular beings with two faces and four legs. Because they were so unruly, Zeus sought to weaken them by dividing them in two. Ever since their division, humans have been *symbola*, longing for their other half, longing for a healing wholeness. The Greek *symbállein* thus means 'to bring together'. Rituals are also symbolic practices, practices of *symbállein*, in the sense that they bring people together and create an alliance, a wholeness, a community.

Symbolism as a medium of community is gradually disappearing. De-symbolization and de-ritualization condition one another. The social anthropologist Mary Douglas notes with amazement:

> One of the gravest problems of our day is the lack of commitment to common symbols. . . . If it were merely a matter of our fragmentation into small groups, each committed to its proper symbolic forms, the case would be simple to understand. But more mysterious is a widespread, explicit rejection of rituals as such. Ritual has become a bad word signifying empty conformity. We are witnessing a revolt against formalism, even against form.[6]

The disappearance of symbols points towards the increasing atomization of society. At the same time, society is becoming increasingly narcissistic. The narcissistic process of internalization develops an aversion to form. Objective forms are avoided in favour of subjective states. Rituals evade narcissistic interiority. The ego-libido

6

cannot attach itself to them. Those who devote themselves to rituals must ignore themselves. Rituals produce a distance from the self, a self-transcendence. They de-psychologize and de-internalize those enacting them.

Symbolic perception is gradually being replaced by a *serial perception* that is incapable of producing the experience of duration. Serial perception, the constant registering of the new, does not linger. Rather, it rushes from one piece of information to the next, from one experience to the next, from one sensation to the next, without ever coming to closure. Watching film series is so popular today because they conform to the habit of serial perception. At the level of media consumption, this habit leads to *binge watching*, to *comatose viewing*. While symbolic perception is *intensive*, serial perception is *extensive*. Because of its extensiveness, serial perception is characterized by shallow attention. Intensity is giving way everywhere to extensity. Digital communication is extensive communication; it does not establish relationships, only connections.

The neoliberal regime pushes serial perception, reinforces the serial habitus. It intentionally abolishes duration in order to drive more consumption. The permanent process of updating, which has now extended to all areas of life, does not permit the development of any duration or allow for any completion. The ever-present compulsion of production leads to a *de-housing* [Enthausung], making life more contingent, transient and unstable. But dwelling requires duration.

Attention deficit disorder results from a pathological intensification of serial perception. Perception is never at rest: it has lost the capacity to linger. The cultural technique of deep attention emerged precisely out of ritual and religious practices. It is no accident that 'religion' is derived from *relegere*: to take note. Every religious practice is an exercise in attention. A temple is a place of the highest degree of attention. According to Malebranche, attention is the natural prayer of the soul. Today, the soul does not pray. It is permanently *producing itself*.

Today, many forms of repetition, such as learning by heart, are scorned on account of the supposed stifling of creativity and innovation they involve. The expression 'to learn something by heart', like the French *apprendre par coeur*, tells us that apparently only repetition reaches the heart. In the face of increasing rates of attention deficit disorder, the introduction of 'ritual studies' as a school subject has recently been advocated as a means of reviving the exercise of ritual repetition as a cultural technique.[7] Repetition stabilizes and deepens attention.

Rituals are characterized by repetition. Repetition differs from routine in its capacity to create intensity. What is the origin of the intensity that characterizes repetition and protects it against becoming routine? For Kierkegaard, repetition and recollection represent the same movement but in opposite directions, 'because what is recollected has already been and is thus repeated backwards, whereas genuine repetition is recollected forwards'.[8] Repetition, as a form of recognition, is therefore a form of completion. Past and present are brought together into a living present. As a form of completion, repetition founds duration and intensity. It ensures that time lingers.

Kierkegaard takes repetition to be opposed to hope as well as to recollection:

Hope is new attire, stiff and starched and splendid. Still, since it has not yet been tried on, one does not know whether it will suit one, or whether it will fit. Recollection is discarded clothing which, however lovely it might be, no longer suits one because one has outgrown it. Repetition is clothing that never becomes worn, that fits snugly and comfortably, that neither pulls nor hangs too loosely.[9]

It is, Kierkegaard writes, 'only the new of which one tires. One never tires of the old.' The old is 'the daily bread that satisfies through blessing'. It *brings happiness*: 'and only a person who does not delude himself that repetition ought to be something new, for then he tires of it, is genuinely happy'.[10]

The daily bread provides no stimuli. Stimuli quickly pale. Repetition discovers intensity in what provides no stimuli, in the unprepossessing, in the *bland*. The person who expects something new and exciting all the time, by contrast, overlooks what is already there. The meaning, that is, the path, can be repeated. You do not grow tired of the path:

I can only repeat something altogether uneventful that was yet accompanied by something in the corner of my eyes that pleased me (the light of the day or the dusk); even a sunset is already event-like and unrepeatable; I cannot even repeat a particular light, or a dusk, but only a *path* (and must be prepared for all the stones on it, even the new ones).[11]

Chasing new stimuli, excitement and experience, we lose the capacity for repetition. The neoliberal dispositifs of authenticity, innovation and creativity involve a permanent compulsion to seek the new, but they ultimately only produce variations of the same. The old, what once was and what allows for a fulfilling repetition, is expunged because it opposes the logic of intensification that pertains to production. Repetition, by contrast, stabilizes life. Its characteristic trait is the 'making at home in the world' [Einhausung].

The new quickly deteriorates into routine. It is a commodity that is used up and arouses the need for the new again. The compulsion to reject routines produces more routines. The temporal logic inherent in the new means that it quickly fades into routine; it does not allow for a fulfilling repetition. The compulsion of production, as the compulsion to seek the new, only gets us deeper into the quagmire of routine. In order to escape routine, to escape emptiness, we consume ever more new things, new stimuli and experiences. It is precisely the feeling of emptiness which spurs communication and consumption. The 'intense life' advertised by the neoliberal regime is in truth simply a life of intense consumption. In the face of an illusory 'intense life', we must consider the possibility that there may be another form of life that is more intense than that of constant consumption and communication.

Rituals bring forth a community in which resonances occur, one that is capable of accord, of a common rhythm:

> Rituals produce sociocultural axes of resonance along which may be experienced three different kinds of resonant relationship: *vertical* (e.g. to the gods, the cosmos, time, or eternity), *horizontal* (within one's social community), and *diagonal* (with respect to *things*).[12]

10

Without resonance we are thrown back on to ourselves, isolated. Increasing narcissism works against the experience of resonance. Resonance is not an echo of the self; the dimension of the other is inherent in it. It means accord. Where resonance disappears completely, depression arises. Today's crisis of community is a crisis of resonance. Digital communication channels are filled with echo chambers in which the voices we hear are mainly our own. Likes, friends and followers do not provide us with resonance; they only strengthen the echoes of the self.

Rituals are processes of embodiment and bodily performances. In them, the valid order and values of a community are physically experienced and solidified. They are written into the body, incorporated, that is, physically internalized. Thus, rituals create a bodily knowledge and memory, an embodied identity, a bodily connection. A ritual community is a *communal body* [Körperschaft], and there is a bodily dimension inherent to community. To the extent that it exerts a disembodying influence, digitalization weakens common ties. Digital communication is disembodied communication.

Ritual acts also include feelings, but the bearer of these feelings is not the isolated individual. In a ritual of mourning, for instance, the mourning is an objective feeling, a collective feeling. It is impersonal. Collective feelings have nothing to do with individual psychology. In a ritual of mourning, the community is the actual subject that mourns. Faced with the experience of loss, the community imposes the mourning upon itself. Such collective feelings consolidate a community. The increasing atomization of society also takes hold of its emotional

11

world. The formation of collective feelings becomes less frequent. Instead, fleeting affects and emotions, the states of isolated individuals, predominate. Unlike emotions and affects, feelings can be collective. Digital communication, however, is predominantly affect based: it tends towards the immediate outpouring of affect. Twitter is an affective medium, and the politics based on it is an affective politics. Politics is reason and mediation; reason, which is time-intensive, is currently being replaced by immediate affect.

The neoliberal regime isolates people while at the same time invoking empathy. Because it is a resonant body, however, ritual community does not require empathy. The demand for empathy can be heard in particular in atomized societies. The present hype surrounding the concept has primarily economic causes: empathy is used as an efficient means of production; it serves the purpose of emotionally influencing and directing people. Under the neoliberal regime, a person is not only exploited during working hours; rather, the whole person is exploited. In this context, emotional management turns out to be more effective than rational management. The former reaches deeper into a person than does the latter. Neoliberal psycho-politics attempts to elicit positive emotions and to exploit them. In the final analysis, it is freedom itself that is here being exploited. In this respect, neoliberal psycho-politics differs from the biopolitics of industrial modernity, which operates through disciplinary compulsion and command.

Digital communication is increasingly developing into communication without community. The neoliberal regime encourages communication without community by isolating everyone as *the producer of him- or herself.* Producing is derived from the Latin verb *producere*, meaning presenting or making visible. Like the French *produire* it still carries the meaning of presenting. *Se produire* means 'to play to the gallery'. The colloquial German expression *sich produzieren* probably has the same etymology. Today, we are constantly and compulsively playing to the gallery. This is especially the case, for instance, on social media: the social is coming to be completely subordinated to self-production. Everyone is producing him- or herself in order to garner more attention. The compulsion of self-production leads to a crisis of community. The so-called 'community'[13] that is today invoked everywhere is an atrophied community, perhaps even a kind of commodified and consumerized community. It lacks the symbolic power to bind people together.

Communication without community can be accelerated because it is additive. Rituals, by contrast, are *narrative processes* that do not allow for acceleration. Symbols *stand still.* This is not the case with information: information *exists* by circulating. *Stillness* only means that communication ceases, stands still. It does not produce anything. In the post-industrial age, the noise of the machines gives way to the noise of communication. More information and more communication holds out the promise of more production. Thus, the compulsion of production expresses itself in the compulsion of communication.

The compulsion of production brings with it the compulsion to perform well. Performance differs from labour in libido-economical terms. In the case of labour, the ego need not take centre stage. In the case of performance, however, the ego relates specifically to itself. It not only produces an object; it produces *itself*. Someone who is absorbed by object-libido does not produce but rather *exhausts him- or herself*. The narcissistic relation to the self constitutes the performance. The ego-libido rules over the performing subject. The better it performs, the more ego it gains. Freud, we know, associated the ego-libido with the death drive. The narcissistic subject of performance breaks apart because of a fatal accumulation of ego-libido. It exploits itself voluntarily and passionately until it breaks down. It optimizes itself to death. Its failing is called depression or burnout.

In a society governed by ritual, there is no depression. In such a society, the soul is fully absorbed by ritual forms; it is even emptied out. Rituals contain aspects of the world, and they produce in us a strong relationship to the world. Depression, by contrast, is based on an excessive relation to self. Wholly incapable of leaving the self behind, of transcending ourselves and relating to the world, we withdraw into our shells. The world disappears. We circle around ourselves, tortured by feelings of emptiness. Rituals, by contrast, disburden the ego of the self, de-psychologizing and de-internalizing the ego.

Hierarchies and power relations are often inscribed in rituals. By means of their aesthetic aspects, rituals can also lend a certain aura to domination. But they are in essence symbolic practices of 'making at home in the world'. Roland Barthes also conceives of rituals and ceremonies from the perspective of 'making at home in the world'. They protect us, he says, against the abysses of being: 'Ceremony . . . protects like a house: something that allows one to live in one's feelings. Example: mourning. . . .' The ceremony of mourning 'acts like a

14

varnish, protects, insulates the skin against the atrocious burns of mourning'.[14] When there are no rituals to act as protective measures, life is wholly unprotected. The compulsion of production cannot cope with this transcendental lack of protection and lack of being at home, which it ultimately exacerbates.[15]

2

The Compulsion of Authenticity

The society of authenticity is a performance society. All members perform themselves. All produce themselves. Everyone pays homage to the cult of the self, the worship of self in which everyone is his or her own priest. Charles Taylor credits the modern cult of authenticity with a 'moral force':

> Being true to myself means being true to my own originality, and that is something only I can articulate and discover. In articulating it, I am also defining myself. I am realizing a potentiality that is properly my own. This is the background understanding to the modern ideal of authenticity, and to the goals of self-fulfilment or self-realization in which it is usually couched. This is the background that gives moral force to the culture of authenticity, including its most degraded, absurd, or trivialized forms.[1]

The creation of self, however, must not be self-centred; it has to take place against the backdrop of a social horizon of meaning that gives the act of self-creation a relevance that transcends the self:

> Only if I exist in a world in which history, or the demands of nature, or the needs of my fellow human beings, or the duties of citizenship, or the call of God, or something else of this order matters crucially, can I define an identity for myself that is not trivial. Authenticity is not the enemy of demands that emanate from beyond the self; it supposes such demands.[2]

From this perspective, authenticity and community are not mutually exclusive. Taylor distinguishes between the form and content of authenticity. Self-referentiality only concerns its form, namely the form of self-fulfilment. According to Taylor, its content, by contrast, must not be self-centred. Authenticity only proves itself insofar as the identity created contains an explicit reference to a community and so is able to hold true independent of one's own self.

Contrary to Taylor's assumptions, however, authenticity is in fact the enemy of community. The narcissism of authenticity undermines community. In terms of its content, what is crucial is not its reference to a community or some other higher order but its market value, which effaces all other values. Thus, the form and content of authenticity coincide: both concern the self. The cult of authenticity shifts the question of identity from society to the individual person. Within the cult of authenticity, the production of self becomes a permanent activity. Authenticity thus atomizes society.

Taylor's moral justification of authenticity ignores that subtle process, within the neoliberal regime, by which the ideas of freedom and self-realization are transformed into vehicles for more efficient exploitation. The neoliberal regime exploits morality. Once it is able to present itself as freedom, domination becomes complete. Authenticity is a neoliberal form of production. You exploit yourself voluntarily in the belief that you are realizing yourself. In the cult of authenticity, the neoliberal regime appropriates the person himself and turns him into a highly efficient site of production. The whole person is incorporated into the production process.

The cult of authenticity is an obvious sign of the decay of the social:

> When some one person is judged to be authentic, or when society as a whole is described as creating problems of human authenticity, the language reveals one way in which social action is being devalued in the process of placing more weight on psychological matters.[3]

The compulsion of authenticity leads to narcissistic introspection, a permanent occupation with one's own psychology. Communication is also organized psychologically. The society of authenticity is a society of intimacy and exposure. The nudism of the soul into which we are encouraged lends society a pornographic character. Social relations are more genuine and authentic the more intimate they are, the more they reveal what was private.

The society of the eighteenth century was still dominated by ritual forms of interaction. The public space resembled a stage, a theatre. The body also represented a stage. It was a dressed puppet without soul, without psychology, that had to be draped and decorated and fitted out with signs and symbols. The wig framed the face like a painting. The fashion itself was theatrical, and people were properly in love with scenic presentations. A lady's coiffure was also designed as a scene, representing either a historical event (*pouf à la circonstance*) or an emotion (*pouf au sentiment*). These emotions, however, did not reflect conditions of the soul. The emotions were mainly *played* with. The face itself became a stage on which various characters were represented with the help of beauty spots (*mouches*). If they were placed at the corner of the eye, they meant passion. Placed on the lower lip, they indicated the frankness of the wearer. The face understood as a stage is utterly remote from that *face* we find presented today on Facebook.

The nineteenth century discovered work, and play became increasingly distrusted. There was now much more work than play: the world resembled a factory rather than a theatre. The culture of theatrical presentation gave way to the culture of interiority. This development can also be seen in fashion. Stage costumes and ordinary clothes began to differ more and more. The theatrical element disappeared from fashion. Europeans started to wear work clothes:

> Never had an age taken itself with more portentous seriousness. Culture ceased to be 'played'. Outward forms were no longer intended to give the appearance, the fiction, if you like, of a higher, ideal mode of life. There

is no more striking symptom of the decline of the play-factor than the disappearance of everything imaginative, fanciful, fantastic from men's dress after the French Revolution.[4]

In the course of the nineteenth century, men's clothes became increasingly homogeneous. They became standardized, like work uniforms. If the condition of a society can be read off its fashion, then the increasingly pornographic nature of fashion reflects an increasingly pornographic society. Today's fashion has obvious pornographic traits; more flesh is displayed than form.

With the rise of the cult of authenticity, tattoos have also become fashionable again. Within a ritual context, they symbolize the alliance between individual and community. In the nineteenth century, when tattoos were very popular, especially among the upper classes, the body was still a surface onto which yearnings and dreams were projected. Today, tattoos lack any symbolic power. All they do is point to the uniqueness of the bearer. The body is neither a ritual stage nor a surface of projection; rather, it is an advertising space. The neoliberal hell of the same is populated with tattooed clones.

The cult of authenticity erodes public space, which disintegrates into private spaces. Everyone carries their own private space with them wherever they go. In public space, one has to leave aside the private and play a role. It is a space for scenic presentations, a theatre. The play, the drama, is essential to it:

Playacting in the form of manners, conventions, and ritual gestures is the very stuff out of which public relations are formed, and from which public relations derive their emotional meaning. The more social conditions erode the public forum, the more are people routinely inhibited from exercising the capacity to playact. The members of an intimate society become artists deprived of an art.[5]

Today, the world is not a theatre in which roles are played and ritual gestures exchanged, but a market in which one exposes and exhibits oneself. Theatrical presentation gives way to a pornographic exhibition of the private.

Sociability and politeness also make major contributions to theatrical presentation. They play with the semblance of beauty, and thus require a scenic, theatrical distance. In the name of authenticity or genuineness, the semblance of beauty, the ritual gesture, is today discarded as something purely external. But this genuineness is, in truth, crudeness and barbarity. The narcissistic cult of authenticity is partly responsible for the increasing brutalization of society. We live in a culture of the affect. Where ritual gestures and manners decay, affect and emotion gain the upper hand. On social media, too, the scenic distance that is constitutive of the public sphere is reduced, and the result is affective communication without distance.

The narcissistic cult of authenticity makes us blind to the symbolic force of forms, which exert a substantial influence on emotion and thought. We may imagine a *ritual turn* that re-establishes the *priority of forms*. It would invert the relationship between inside and outside, spirit and body. *The body moves the spirit, not vice versa. Body does not follow spirit, but spirit follows body.* We may also say: *the medium produces the message.* This is the *force of ritual.*

21

External forms lead to internal changes. Thus, ritual forms of politeness have mental effects. The semblance of beauty produces a beautiful soul, not vice versa:

> Polite behaviour can strongly influence our thoughts. And miming graciousness, kindness and happiness is of considerable help in combating ill humor and even stomach aches; the movements involved – gracious gestures and smiles – do this much good: they exclude the possibility of contrary movements, which express rage, defiance, and sadness. That is why social activities, visits, formal occasions, and parties are so well liked. It is a chance to imitate happiness; and this kind of comedy certainly frees us from tragedy – no small accomplishment.[6]

Politeness is an *as-if ritual*. Culture as such is made up of *as-if rituals*. If we remove the as-if gestures in the name of authenticity or genuineness, we destroy the element of civilization:

> Again, in order to feel kindly towards a person to whom we have been inimical, the only way is more or less deliberately to smile, to make sympathetic inquiries, and to force ourselves to say genial things. One hearty laugh together will bring enemies into a closer communion of heart than hours spent on both sides in inward wrestling with the mental demon of uncharitable feeling. To wrestle with a bad feeling only pins our attention on it, and keeps it still fastened in the mind; whereas if we act as if from some better feeling, the old bad feeling soon folds its tent like an Arab and silently steals away.[7]

A ritual of politeness is not an expression of subjective feeling; it is an objective act. It resembles a magical invocation that produces a positive mental state.

The culture of authenticity goes hand in hand with the distrust of ritualized forms of interaction. Only spontaneous emotion, that is, a subjective state, is authentic. Behaviour that has been *formed* in some way is denigrated as inauthentic or superficial. In the society of authenticity, actions are guided internally, motivated psychologically, whereas in ritual societies actions are determined by externalized forms of interaction. Rituals make the world objective; they mediate our relation to the world. The compulsion of authenticity, by contrast, makes everything subjective, thereby intensifying narcissistic tendencies. Today, narcissistic disorders are on the rise because we are increasingly losing the ability to conduct social interactions outside the boundaries of the self. The narcissistic *homo psychologicus* is captivated by itself, caught in an intricate inwardness. What results is a poverty in world, with the self simply circling around itself. Thus, *homo psychologicus* falls into a depression.

In a culture of raging narcissism, playfulness disappears, and life loses its cheerfulness and exuberance. The culture retreats from that holy sphere of play. The compulsions of work and performance intensify the profanation of life. The holy seriousness of play gives way to the profane seriousness of work.

James Bond movies also reflect this development. They have become more serious and less playful over time. The most recent ones even forgo the depiction of rituals of carefree love at the end. The final scene of *Skyfall* has a disturbing effect in this regard; Bond, instead of dedicating himself to amorous play, simply receives his next assignment from his superior, M. M. says to Bond: 'Lots to be done. Are you ready to get back to work?' A stern-faced Bond replies: 'With pleasure, M. ... with pleasure.'

The ritual spaces that make possible playful and ceremonial exuberance have been eroded. They have become spaces of excess and extravagance that stand out against profane everyday life. Culture has been made profane. Films like *La Grande Bouffe* would today only be met with incomprehension. Transgression is a general feature of celebratory ritual:

> It [i.e. culture] orders and creates exceptional celebratory situations in which what may usually be denied now suddenly seems called for and can be experienced in ceremonies of transgression as cheerful sociability, as joyful triumph, or even as wild enthusiasm. Totemistic societies that prohibited the eating of certain animals provide a striking example (one with which Freud was familiar). On a particular day of the year, the prohibition is lifted and instead it is commanded that, on that day, the totem feast must be held – a joyful occasion.[8]

The profanation of culture brings about its disenchantment. Today, the arts are also increasingly rendered profane and disenchanted. Magic and enchantment – the true sources of art – disappear from culture, to be replaced by discourse. The enchanting exterior is replaced with the true interior, the magic signifier with the profane signified. The place of compelling, captivating forms is taken by discursive content. Magic gives way to *transpar-*

ency. The imperative of transparency fosters an animosity to form. Art becomes *transparent* with regard to its meaning. It no longer seduces. The magic veil is cast off. The forms do not themselves *talk*. The language of forms, of signifiers, is characterized by compression, complexity, equivocation, exaggeration, a high degree of ambiguity that even reaches the level of contradiction. These suggest *meaningfulness* without immediately being reducible to meaning. All these now disappear, and instead we are confronted with simplified claims and messages that are artificially imposed on the work of art.

The disenchantment of art makes it Protestant in nature. It is de-ritualized, as it were, and stripped of its splendid forms:

> Until the end of the 1980s, the spaces in which art was displayed still looked like Catholic churches, full of colourful forms and exuberant shapes. Since then, art societies seem to have become deeply Protestant, focusing on content and the spoken or written word.[9]

Art is not a discourse. It produces its effects through forms and signifiers, and not through the signified. The process of internalization destroys the arts, bringing them closer to discourse and forsaking the mysterious outside for the profane inside. The disenchantment of art is a symptom of narcissism, of narcissistic internalization.

Collective narcissism reduces Eros and disenchants the world. The erotic resources of culture dry up. These resources are also the forces that hold a community together and inspire it to play and to hold festivals. Without them, society becomes atomized. Rituals and ceremonies are the genuinely human acts which allow life to appear to be an enchanting, celebratory affair. Their disappearance desecrates and profanes, transforming life into mere survival. We might thus expect *a re-enchantment of the world* to create a healing power that could counteract collective narcissism.

3

Rituals of Closure

In a present characterized by an excess of openings and dissolving boundaries, we are losing the capacity for closure, and this means that life is becoming a purely additive process. For something to die, life must find its own closure. If life is deprived of any possibility of closure, it will end in non-time. Because it rushes from one sensation to the next, even perception is now incapable of closure. Only contemplative lingering is capable of closure. The closure of the eyes is emblematic of contemplative closure. The flood of images and information makes closure of the eyes impossible. In the absence of the negativity of closure, what emerges is an endless addition and accumulation of the same, an excess of positivity, an excrescent proliferation of information and communication. Where everything is connected, no closure is possible. The loss of forms of completion that accompanies overproduction and overconsumption leads to systemic collapse.

The neoliberal imperative of optimization and performance does not allow for any completion. Everything is provisional and incomplete; nothing is final and conclusive. It is not only computer software that is subject to the compulsion of optimization. All areas of life are subordinated to its dictates, even education. Life-long learning does not involve completion. It amounts only to life-long production. The neoliberal regime abolishes all forms of closure and completion in the name of increased productivity. The *We* that is capable of joint action is also a form of closure. Today, it disintegrates into egos who voluntarily exploit themselves as entrepreneurs of their own selves. Ties and bonds, as forms of closure, are also increasingly cut. Flexibility is enforced by the ruthless destruction of bonds. The isolated subject of performance exploits itself most efficiently when it remains open to everything – in other words, when it is flexible.

The inability to bring about closure is connected with narcissism. The narcissistic subject feels itself most intensely not in what it does, in the work completed, but in ongoing performance. What is done, what is completed, exists as an independent, finished object, something independent of the producing subject's self. Thus, the subject avoids bringing anything to completion:

Continual escalation of expectations so that present behavior is never fulfilling is a lack of 'closure'. The sense of having reached a goal is avoided because the experiences would be then objectified; they would have a shape, a form, and so exist independently of oneself.

... Thus the quality of a narcissistic impulse is that it must be a continual subjective state.[1]

The excessive opening up and removal of boundaries is present at all levels of society. It is the imperative of neoliberalism. Globalization also dissolves all closed structures in order to accelerate the circulation of capital, commodities and information. It removes boundaries, de-sites [ent-ortet] the world, turning it into a global market. A site [Ort] is a form of closure. The global market is an off-site [Ab-Ort]. Digital networks also abolish sites. The Internet is an off-site, too. It is not possible to dwell in it. We surf the net. Tourists also travel through the de-sited world. They circulate incessantly, like commodities and information.[2]

In his essay *Behutsame Ortsbestimmung* [A careful definition of a place], the Hungarian writer Péter Nádas describes a village with an ancient wild pear tree at its centre as a ritually closed place: 'Ever since I have lived near this gigantic wild pear tree, I have not needed to go yonder when I want to look into the distance or back in time.'[3] The village represents a closed order. It makes lingering possible. Thus, you do not need to go 'yonder'. The old wild pear tree is a centre of gravity that creates a deep unity among the people. It is where the villagers meet and sing: 'On warm summer nights, quiet singing can be heard from under the wild pear. The villagers sang quietly. They probably did not want to behave inappropriately and disturb the night.'[4] There is not much to communicate in this place, and so no communicative noise disturbs the silence:

29

You get the feeling that life here does not consist of personal experiences . . . but of a deep keeping of silence. That is understandable, however, given that a human being blessed with individual consciousness is permanently forced to say more than he knows, whereas in a pre-modern environment everyone says much less than everyone knows.[5]

Under the pear tree, the villager indulges in 'ritual contemplation', a ritual silence, and gives his blessing to the 'content of collective consciousness'.[6] The rituals of closure stabilize the village. They produce a *cognitive mapping*, something that is dissolved in the course of digitization and globalization.[7]

The villagers are deeply attached to each other. Perception, as well as action, takes on a collective form: seeing and hearing take place in common. Actions are not assigned to a specific subject:

When the village does something or perceives something, neither action nor perception are those of a subject, a person; that is, the people involved in an action or perception are ritually subsumed and their experiences are assigned to the generic name that stands for the place.[8]

Collective consciousness creates a community without communication. For the villagers, there is one story, continuously repeated, and this story is the *world*: 'They do not have opinions on this or that, but incessantly tell just one great story.'[9] There is a *tacit* agreement in the village, and nobody disturbs this agreement with their personal experiences or opinions. No one tries to be heard or to attract attention. Attention is primarily directed at the community itself. The ritual community is a community of common listening and belonging, a community in the quiet unity of silence. Where such primordial closeness disappears, excessive communication takes its place. Community without communication gives way to communication without community.

A narrative is a form of closure: it has a beginning and an end and is characterized by a closed order. Information, by contrast, is additive, not narrative. It does not combine into a story, a song, that could form the basis of meaning and identity. Information can only be endlessly accumulated. Beneath the old wild pear tree, silence rules, because everything has already been told. Today, the noise of communication replaces the silence. The quietly wistful final line of *Behutsame Ortsbestimmung* reads: 'Today, there are no chosen trees, and the song of the village has faded.'[10]

The title of the second essay in *Behutsame Ortsbestimmung* is 'Der eigene Tod' ['One's own death']. In it, Nádas describes his own near-death experience. Here, death ends in a birth. It is a form of closure. Death, understood in this way, is not an end, not a loss. It is imagined as a new beginning. The death canal, at the end of which a bright light can be seen, becomes the birth canal:

I slipped out of my mother's womb . . . The oval opening was formed by my mother's large widened labia, which I know from the perspective of the birth canal, the great labia of my mother, who died decades ago,

31

how they were widened, or became more and more stretched because I came closer in order to be born.[11]

The hour of death turns into the hour of birth. Thus, there emerges a cyclical *connection between death and birth*, which creates an *infinity*. Human life is seen as analogous to that cyclical time embodied by the wild pear tree. The essay 'Der eigene Tod' is itself literally enclosed by more than 150 photographs of the old wild pear tree. We know that Nádas, as if obsessed, took photos of the tree in all seasons. Taking photographs, in this case, is a ritual of closure. The photographs create a peculiar temporal feeling, a cyclical time, meaning a time that is *closed in itself*.

Nádas's village is probably not a friendly site. We should not expect to find hospitality in an archaic collective. Given the possibility of violence associated with a fundamentalist closure of sites, it would be naive to believe that closure is invariably positive. The revival of nationalism today has in part to do with an urge for a kind of closure that involves the exclusion of the other, of the stranger. We should not forget, however, that both the negativity of total closure and the positivity of excessive opening are forms of violence that lead to counter-violence.

Human beings are creatures of sites [Ortswesen]. Dwelling, staying, is only possible where there is a site. But a creature of sites is not necessarily a site fundamentalist [Ortsfundamentalist]. Being a creature of sites does not rule out hospitality. The destructive de-siting of the world by the global smooths out all differences and permits only variations of the same. Otherness, the foreign, inhibits production. Thus, the global produces a *hell of the same*. It is this violence of the global, in particular, that stirs up site fundamentalism.

Culture is a form of closure, and so founds an identity. However, culture is not an excluding but an *including identity*. It is therefore receptive of what is foreign. Regarding the genesis of Greek culture, Hegel remarks: 'We have just spoken of heterogeneity [Fremdartigkeit] as an element of the Greek Spirit, and it is well known that the rudiments of Greek civilization are connected with the advent of foreigners.' With 'grateful recollection', he says, the Greeks preserved the arrival of the foreigners in their mythology.[12] Prometheus, for instance, originates from the Caucasus. According to Hegel, it is 'a superficial and absurd idea that such a beautiful and truly free life can be produced by a process so incomplex as the development of a race keeping within the limits of blood-relationship and friendship'. Rather, it is 'its inherent heterogeneity [Fremdartigkeit in sich selbst], through which alone it [that is, the spirit; B.-C. H.] acquires the power of realizing itself as Spirit'.[13] Spirit is a closure, an enclosing power which, however, incorporates the other, the foreign. The 'inherent heterogeneity' is constitutive of the formation of spirit. Inasmuch as it mindlessly excludes what is foreign, the idea of the *Leitkultur* [dominant culture], often invoked today, is devoid of spirit. As a form of *Retrotopia*, it is situated in the realm of the imaginary.[14]

Globalization de-sites culture. It perforates the boundaries of cultural spaces, collapsing them into a hyper-culture: cultural spaces overlap and penetrate each other in juxtaposition without distance.[15] A *hyper-market of culture* emerges. Hyper-culture is a formula for cultural consumption. Culture is offered in commodity form.

Like a rhizome, it spreads without boundaries, without centre. Nádas's wild pear tree is precisely a symbol of a sited culture. It is the opposite of a rhizome. A de-sited hyper-culture is additive; it is not a form of closure:

> The tree is filiation, but the rhizome is alliance, uniquely alliance. The tree imposes the verb 'to be', but the fabric of the rhizome is the conjunction, 'and . . . and . . . and . . .'. This conjunction carries enough force to shake and uproot the verb 'to be'.[16]

Being is the *verb for a site*. The *hyper-cultural logic of the And* sublates it. The endless conjunction celebrated by Deleuze is ultimately destructive. It leads to a cancerous proliferation of the same, even to the hell of the same.

The cultural hyper-market does not contain the foreign. It escapes consumption. The global is not a site for spirit because spirit requires 'inherent heterogeneity'. What is foreign enlivens, even inspires, spirit. The strengthening of site fundamentalism, the *Leitkultur*, is a reaction to the global, neoliberal hyper-culture, to hyper-cultural non-sitedness. The two cultural formations confront each other in hostile and irreconcilable opposition, but they have one thing in common: they exclude what is foreign.

Most of all, the abolition of rituals removes autonomous time [Eigenzeit]. This time is familiar to us from the various stages of life:

> We are all familiar with this autonomous time [Eigenzeit, D. S.], as we may call it, from our own experience of life: childhood, youth, maturity, old age, and death are all

basic forms of such autonomous time. . . . The time that allows us to be young or old is not clock time at all, and there is obviously something discontinuous about it.[17]

Rituals give form to the essential transitions of life. They are forms of closure. Without them, *we slip through*. Thus, we age without growing *old*, or we remain infantile consumers who never become adults. The discontinuity of autonomous time gives way to the continuity of production and consumption.

Rites of passage give structure to life in the same way seasons do. Whoever passes a certain threshold has concluded a phase of life and enters into a new one. Thresholds, as transitions, give a rhythm to, articulate, and even narrate space and time. They make possible a deep experience of order. Thresholds are temporally intense transitions. Today, they are being erased and replaced by an accelerated and seamless communication and production. This is making us poorer in space and time. In our attempt to *produce* more space and time, we lose them. They lose their *language* and become *mute*. Thresholds *speak*. Thresholds *transform*. Beyond a threshold, there is what is *other*, what is *foreign*. In the absence of the imagination of the threshold, the magic of the threshold, all that is left is the *hell of the same*. The construction of the global is premised on the ruthless destruction of thresholds and transitions. Information and commodities prefer a world without thresholds: *unresisting smoothness* accelerates circulation. Today, temporally intense transitions are disintegrating into speedy passages, continuous links and endless clicks.

35

4

Festivals and Religion

God blessed and sanctified the seventh day. The rest enjoyed on the Sabbath consecrates the work of creation. It is not mere idleness. Rather, it is an essential part of creation. In his commentary on the Book of Genesis, Rashi thus remarks: 'After the six days of creation, what was still missing from the universe? *Menuchah* [inoperativity, rest]. The Sabbath came, the *menuchah* came, and the universe was complete.'[1] Sabbath rest does not follow creation; it brings creation to completion. Without it, the creation would be incomplete. God does not rest on the seventh day simply to recover from the work he has done. Rather, rest is his nature. It completes the creation. It is the essence of the creation. Thus, when we subordinate rest to work, we ignore the divine.

For Franz Rosenzweig, the Sabbath is 'the holiday of the Creation',[2] a 'holiday of resting and of closely reflecting',[3] a 'holiday of completion'.[4] Most importantly, during the Sabbath man rests 'his tongue from the everyday chit-chat and learns silence and listening'.[5] The Sabbath demands silence; the mouth must be closed. Silent listening unites a people and creates a community without communication:

> for we are united only in silence; the word unites, but those who are united grow silent – therefore the burning mirror that collects the sunbeams of eternity in the tiny cycle of the year, the liturgy, must introduce man into this silence. In the liturgy too of course the mutual silence can only be that which is last, and all that precedes is only the preparatory school for this that comes last. In such an education, the word still rules. The word itself must guide man in so that he may learn to grow mutually silent. The beginning of this education is that he may learn to listen.[6]

The divine commands silence: 'The verb *myein*, "to initiate", means etymologically, "to close" – notably the eyes, but, more importantly, the mouth. At the beginning of the sacred rites, the herald would "command silence" (*epitattei ten siopen*).'[7] The silence gives rise to listening. It is accompanied by a special receptivity, by a deep, contemplative attentiveness. Today's compulsion of communication means that we can close neither our eyes nor our mouths. It desecrates life.

In the digital world, where attention has a flat structure, silence and muteness have no place. Silence and muteness require a vertical structure, but digital communication is horizontal. In digital communication, nothing *protrudes*. Nothing *deepens*. It is not intensive but extensive, and this leads to an increase in communicative noise. Because we cannot remain silent, we must communicate. Or: we cannot remain silent because we are subject to the compulsion of communication, the compulsion of production. The liberation and emancipation from the word brought about by silence turns back into the compulsion of communication. Freedom reverts back into compulsion.

Silence is essential to festivals not only in the Jewish religion but in religion in general.[8] It produces a particular intensity of life:

> And yet rest, as opposed to the commotion of everyday life, is part of the essence of the festival: a silence in which the intensity of life and contemplation are united, that can even still unite them when the intensity of life grows into exuberance.[9]

We have today entirely lost the capacity for the kind of rest proper to the festival, one that is characterized by both the intensity of life and the intensity of contemplation. Life reaches a true intensity at the very moment the *vita activa* (which in its late modern crisis degenerates into hyperactivity) incorporates the *vita contemplativa*.

Rest belongs to the sphere of the sacred. Work, by contrast, is a profane activity that must be wholly absent from the religious act. Rest and work represent two fundamentally different existential forms. They are divided by an *ontological*, even a *theological*, *difference*. Rest is not merely recovery from work, nor is it a preparation for further work. Rather, it transcends work, and it must in no way come into contact with work:

> This is because work is an eminent form of profane activity: it has no other apparent end than to provide for the temporal necessities of life; it puts us in relations with ordinary things only. On feast days, on the contrary, the religious life attains an exceptional degree of intensity. So the contrast between the two forms of existence is especially marked at this moment; consequently, they cannot remain near to each other. A man cannot approach his god intimately while he still bears on him marks of his profane life; inversely, he cannot return to his usual occupations when a rite has just sanctified him. So the ritual day of rest is only one particular case of the general incompatibility separating the sacred from the profane.[10]

If rest becomes a form of recovery from work, as is the case today, it loses its specific ontological value. It no longer represents an independent, higher form of existence and degenerates into a derivative of work. Today's compulsion of production perpetuates work and thus eliminates that sacred silence. Life becomes entirely profane, desecrated.

As part of the sphere of the profane, work individualizes and isolates human beings. Festivals, by contrast, unite them. The circular nature of the festival is grounded in the fact that, as essentially collective beings, humans regularly feel the need to unite. The circularity of the festival corresponds to the continual alternation between work and rest, dispersal and assembly:

39

The essential constituent of the cult is the cycle of feasts which return regularly at determined epochs. We are now able to understand whence this tendency towards periodicity comes; the rhythm which the religious life follows only expresses the rhythm of the social life, and results from it. Society is able to revivify the sentiment it has of itself only by assembling. But it cannot be assembled all the time. The exigencies of life do not allow it to remain in congregation indefinitely; so it scatters, to assemble anew when it again feels the need of this. It is to these necessary alternations that the regular alternations of sacred and profane times correspond. . . . Moreover, this rhythm is capable of varying in different societies. Where the period of dispersion is long, and the dispersion itself is extreme, the period of congregation, in its turn, is very prolonged.[11]

As forms of play, festivals are self-representations of life. They are characterized by an excess, an expression of an overflowing life that does not aim at a goal. This is what lies behind their intensity. They are an intense form of life. In the festival, life relates to itself instead of subordinating itself to external purposes. Thus, time that is completely dominated by the compulsion of production, the sort of time we inhabit today, is a time without festival. Life becomes impoverished; it freezes into mere survival.

We *celebrate* [begehen wir] a festival, but it is not possible to celebrate work [die Arbeit zu begehen].[12] We are able to celebrate [begehen] a festival because it *stands* there, as though it were a building. The time of the festival is a time *standing still*. It does not pass or run out. It thus makes *lingering* possible. Time as a sequence of transient, fleeting moments is suspended. There is no goal one *walks towards* [hingehen], and it is precisely *walking towards* that lets time pass. The celebration [Begehen] of a festival suspends transience [Vergehen]. The everlasting [Unvergängliches] is inherent to the festival. The time of a festival is exalted time [Hoch-Zeit].[13] The festival is also the origin of art: 'The essence of our temporal experience of art is in learning how to tarry in this way. And perhaps it is the only way that is granted to us finite beings to relate to what we call eternity.'[14] It is the *essence of art* that it affords life durability: 'That "something can be held in our hesitant stay" – this is what art has always been and still is today.'[15] The compulsion of work erodes life's durability. The time of work is a time that passes, that runs out. If the time of life fully coincides with the time of work, as is the case today, then life itself becomes radically transient.

For Hölderlin, the festival is a 'bridal festival', an exalted time humans spend with the gods. During festivals, humans come close to the gods. A festival founds a community among humans and between humans and gods: it allows humans to participate in the divine. It brings forth intensities. The gods embody precisely the intensities of human life. Life that exhausts itself in work and production is an absolutely atrophied life.

Exalted time [Hoch-Zeit] is also the temporality of schools of higher education [Hoch-Schule]. In ancient Greek, 'school' is *scholé*, that is, leisure. Schools of higher education would thus be schools of higher leisure. Today, they are no longer places of high leisure. They have become places of production, factories of human capital.

They pursue professional training rather than formative education [Bildung]. Formative education is not a means to an end but an end in itself. Through formative education spirit relates to itself instead of subordinating itself to an external purpose.

The university of the Middle Ages was anything but a place to receive professional training. It was a place of ritual. Sceptres, seals, doctoral caps, chains of office and gowns were the accoutrements of academic ritual. Today, universities are abandoning rituals. The modern university, understood as a business that has to serve its customers, no longer has any need for them. Rituals conflict with work and production, and where they are nevertheless re-introduced they are purely decorative and impotent: they are simply opportunities to take selfies or revel in one's own achievements. Where everything is subordinated to production, ritual disappears.

Today's ceremonies or festivals have little to do with exalted time. They are part of the domain of event management.[16] The event, the consumerist form of festival, possesses an altogether different temporal structure, as can be seen in the Latin word *eventus*, meaning 'suddenly coming to the fore'. The temporality of the event is that of the eventuality. It is accidental, arbitrary and non-committal. Rituals and festivals, however, are anything but contingent and non-committal. Eventuality is the temporality of the contemporary society of the event. It is opposed to the binding and committal nature of the festival. In contrast to festivals, events do not create communities. Today's popular festivals have become mass events, and masses are not communities.

The neoliberal regime totalizes production, subordinating all areas of life to its dictates. The totalization of production leads to the total profanation of life. Rest, too, is made to serve production and is degraded into leisure and recreational time. It is no longer the beginning of a holy period of assembly. For some, leisure time is empty time, and this gives rise to a *horror vacui*. The mounting pressure to perform makes even recreational pauses impossible. Thus, many people find that they fall ill during leisure time. This illness has even been given a name: *leisure sickness*.[17] Here, leisure time, a time empty of work, becomes a torment. Active, ritual silence gives way to tormenting idleness.

Work has a beginning and an end. A period of work is followed by a period of rest. Performance, by contrast, has neither an end nor a beginning. There is no period of performance. The neoliberal imperative of performance makes work perpetual. In ritual societies, as Durkheim remarks, collective life sometimes takes on an excessive form, a kind of frenzy, when the period of work, that is, the period of dispersion, is too long or too extreme. Festival is followed by festival. Today, it is work that has become frenzied, and the need for festival and assembly is not felt. Thus, the compulsion of production leads to the disintegration of community.

Capitalism is often interpreted as a religion. However, if religion is understood in terms of *religare*, as something that binds, then capitalism is anything but a religion because it lacks any force to assemble, to create community. Money, by itself, has an individualizing and isolating effect. It increases my individual freedom by liberating me from any personal bond with others. I can have someone else work for me by paying her, and this avoids entering into a personal relationship. And what is essential to religion is contemplative rest, but this is the antithesis of capital. Capital never rests. It is its nature that it must always work and continue moving. To the extent that they lose the capacity for contemplative rest, humans conform to capital. The distinction between the sacred and the profane is also an essential characteristic of religion. The sacred unites those things and values that give vitality to a community. The formation of community is its essential trait. Capitalism, by contrast, erases the distinction between the sacred and the profane by totalizing the profane. It makes everything comparable to everything else and thus equal to everything else. Capitalism brings forth a *hell of the same*.

The religion of Christianity is to a large extent narrative. Festivals such as Easter, Whitsun and Christmas are key narrative moments within an overall narrative which provides meaning and orientation. Every day is given a narrative tension, is made meaningful, by the overall narrative. Time itself becomes narrative, that is, meaningful. Capitalism lacks narrativity. It does not narrate anything [erzählt nichts]; it merely counts [zählt]. It deprives time of all meaningfulness. Time is profaned, reduced to labour time. Thus, all days resemble each other.

By equating capitalism and religion, Agamben puts pilgrims and tourists on the same plane: 'To the faithful in the Temple – the pilgrims who would travel across the earth from temple to temple, from sanctuary to sanctuary – correspond today the tourists who restlessly travel in a world that has been abstracted into a Museum.'[18] In reality, pilgrims and tourists belong to entirely separate orders. Tourists travel through non-sites emptied of

44

meaning, while pilgrims are bound to *sites* that assemble and connect human beings. The assembly is the characteristic trait of sites:

> The site gathers unto itself, supremely and in the extreme. Its gathering power penetrates and pervades everything. The site, the gathering power, gathers in and preserves all it has gathered, not like an encapsulating shell but rather by penetrating with its light all it has gathered, and only thus releasing it into its own nature.[19]

A church is also a place for assembly. *Synagogue* is derived from the Greek *synagein*, meaning, like *symbállein*, to bring together. A church is a site where religious rituals are performed in common, that is, where, together with others, one pays attention to the sacred. Religion as *religare* is at the same time *relegere*, a being attentive. In this way, the temple differs from the museum. Museum visitors and tourists do not form communities. They are masses or crowds. Sites, too, are profaned; they are reduced to sights. *To have seen* is the formula of consumption relating to *relegere*. It does not indicate a deep form of attention. A sight differs fundamentally from the site which shines through what is assembled and releases it into its own nature. Sights do not possess that deep symbolic power which creates a community. Sights are places *one passes by*. They do not permit any *lingering* or *staying*.

   In the face of the intensifying compulsion of production and performance, finding a way to make a different, playful use of life is a political task. Life regains its playful element when it relates to itself instead of subordinating itself to an external purpose. What must be won back is contemplative rest. If our life is deprived of all its contemplative elements, we become suffocated by our own activity. The fact that contemplative rest, silence, is essential to religion is suggested by the existence of the Sabbath. In this way, religion is diametrically opposed to capitalism. *Capitalism dislikes silence.* Silence would be the degree zero of production and, in the post-industrial age, the degree zero of communication.

5

A Game of Life and Death

The glory of play goes along with sovereignty, where sovereignty simply means being free from necessity, from purpose and utility. Sovereignty reveals a soul 'which stands aloof from caring about utility'.[1] The compulsion of production destroys sovereignty as a form of life. Sovereignty gives way to a new kind of *subordination* which, however, masquerades as freedom. The neoliberal subject of performance is an *absolute slave* insofar as, in the absence of a master, it voluntarily exploits itself.

Bataille distinguishes between two types of play, strong and weak. In a society in which utility has become the dominant principle only weak play is deemed acceptable. Weak play fits into the logic of production because it serves the purpose of recreation, time away from work. Strong play, by contrast, cannot be reconciled with the principle of work and production. It puts life itself at risk. It is characterized by sovereignty.

Bataille refers to a ritual in the Indian province of Quilcare discussed by James George Frazer in *The Golden Bough*:

> The festival at which the king of Calicut staked his crown and his life on the issue of battle was known as the 'Great Sacrifice'. It fell every twelfth year . . . the ceremony was observed with great pomp at the Tirunavayi temple, on the north bank of the Ponnani River. The spot is close to the present railway line. As the train rushes by, you can just catch a glimpse of the temple, almost hidden behind a clump of trees on the river bank. From the western gateway of the temple a perfectly straight road, hardly raised above the level of the surrounding rice-fields and shaded by a fine avenue, runs for half a mile to a high ridge with a precipitous bank, on which the outlines of three or four terraces can still be traced. On the topmost of these terraces the king took his stand on the eventful day. The view which it commands is a fine one. Across the flat expanse of the rice-fields, with the broad placid river winding through them, the eye ranges eastward to high tablelands, their lower slopes embowered in woods, while afar off looms the great chain of the western Ghauts, and in the furthest distance the Neilgherries or Blue Mountains, hardly distinguishable from the azure of the sky above.
>
> But it was not to the distant prospect that the king's eyes naturally turned at this crisis of his fate. His attention was arrested by a spectacle nearer at hand. For all the plain below was alive with troops, their banners waving gaily in

the sun, the white tents of their many camps standing sharply out against the green and gold of the rice-fields. Forty thousand fighting men or more were gathered there to defend the king. But if the plain swarmed with soldiers, the road that cuts across it from the temple to the king's stand was clear of them. Not a soul was stirring on it. Each side of the way was barred by palisades, and from the palisades on either hand a long hedge of spears, held by strong arms, projected into the empty road, their blades meeting in the middle and forming a glittering arch of steel. All was now ready. The king waved his sword. At the same moment a great chain of massy gold, enriched with bosses, was placed on an elephant at his side. That was the signal. On the instant a stir might be seen half a mile away at the gate of the temple. A group of swordsmen, decked with flowers and smeared with ashes, has stepped out from the crowd. They have just partaken of their last meal on earth, and they now receive the last blessings and farewells of their friends. A moment more and they are coming down the lane of spears, hewing and stab-bing right and left at the spearmen, winding and turning and writhing among the blades as if they had no bones in their bodies. It is all in vain. One after the other they fall, some nearer the king, some farther off, content to die, not for the shadow of a crown, but for the mere sake of approving their dauntless valour and swordsmanship to the world. On the last days of the festival the same mag-nificent display of gallantry, the same useless sacrifice of life was repeated again and again.[2]

We find this archaic ritual disconcerting because it embodies a form of life that rests on expenditure and play. It is diametrically opposed to our form of life, which is dominated by work and production. To a society that declares bare life sacred, this ritual appears as pure madness, as a theatre of cruelty. A society obsessed with production does not have any access to strong play, to death as an intensity of life. In this archaic society, more is sacrificed than is produced. *Sacrificium* denotes the creation of sacred things. The sacred presupposes a de-production [Ent-Produktion]. The totalization of production desecrates life.

Those archaic warriors are not soldiers. 'Soldier', taken literally, means 'the one who is in someone's pay'. He is a servant. Thus, as opposed to the sovereign warrior, a player, he is afraid of death. He risks his life because he receives payment for it. The soldier, as a mercenary, is a wage earner, a worker, an employee. He does not play. He trades his life. Strong play, whose principle is sovereignty, does not fit into the society of production, which aims at utility, performance and efficiency, and which declares bare life, survival, the continuation of a healthy life, to be an absolute value. Strong play suspends the economy of work and production. Death is not a loss, not a failure, but an expression of the utmost vitality, force and desire.

The society of production is dominated by the fear of death. Capital acts like a guarantee against death. It is imagined to be accumulated time because money allows you to have others work for you, that is, to buy time. Infinite capital creates the illusion of an infinite time. Capital works against death as absolute loss. It is meant to suspend the temporal limits of a life. Bataille suspects that behind the compulsion of accumulation lies the fear of death:

A rich industrialist would laugh or respond by politely shrugging his shoulders if we told him that the truth of a poem is *strong* and altogether sovereign, compared to his voluminous portfolio of shares whose *weak* truth is made up of the fear that subjugates the world to work – made up of that universal degradation imposed by the fear of death.[3]

The banishment of death from life is constitutive of capitalist production. Death is meant to be *produced away*. An antidote against the compulsion of production is therefore the *symbolic exchange* with death: 'The removal of death from life, that is the very operation of the economic – it leaves a *residual* life which can from now on be read in the operational terms of calculation and value. . . . Life returned to death: the very operation of the symbolic.'[4] Archaic societies do not make a sharp distinction between life and death. Death is an aspect of life, and life is only possible in symbolic exchange with death. Rituals of initiation and sacrifice are symbolic acts which regulate numerous transitions from life to death. Initiation is a second birth, following upon death, that is, the end of a phase of life. The relationship between life and death is characterized by reciprocity. Festivals as expenditure imply a symbolic exchange with death: '*Symbolic* death, which has not undergone the *imaginary* disjunction of life and death which is at the origin of the *reality* of death, is exchanged in a social ritual of feasting.'[5] The age of production is accordingly a time without festival. It is dominated by an irreversibility, that of endless growth.

Today, there are hardly any personalities with lives characterized by sovereignty, by a passion for play. The film director Werner Schroeter was one such character. His last film, *La Nuit de chien*, stages strong play, sovereignty, pure expenditure. When asked in an interview about the 'utopian forms' constructed in his film and where they could be found, Schroeter replied:

> In death. In the freedom to choose death. The beauty of the film lies in the fact that I realize this with grandeur – rather than serving it up flimsily, as crumbled cake, like many of my compatriots do these days. This psychological rummaging around in the nitty-gritty – and then, perhaps, grandma has an orgasm one more time. No, that is a different world. My whole life is a utopia because I constantly live in hope. I think positively; that is also why I have survived my illness so far, surprisingly. I was shooting in Porto for nine weeks, with enormous energy: every night, from six in the evening until six in the morning. An enormous physical effort. I fatalistically expose myself to situations, but I am not soft, not with myself and not with others. That is why this can be successful: that one can conquer the fear of death. That fear is not part of my world. I can't even remember when it left me.[6]

In his film, Schroeter develops a utopia in which death represents an intensity, an intensive form of life. It is pure expenditure, an expression of sovereignty.

Michel Foucault was deeply impressed by Werner Schroeter's films, and this led to a conversation between the two on the topics of eroticism and passion, death and suicide. Schroeter describes the freedom unto death as an anarchist feeling: 'I have no fear of death. It's perhaps arrogant to say it but it's the truth. ... To look death in the face is an anarchist feeling dangerous to established society.'[7] Sovereignty, the freedom unto death, is threatening to a society that is organized around work and production, that tries to increase human capital by biopolitical means. That utopia is anarchist insofar as it represents a radical break with a form of life that declares pure life, continued existence, sacred. Suicide is the most radical rejection imaginable of the society of production. *It challenges the system of production*. It represents the *symbolic exchange with death* which undoes the separation of death from life brought about by capitalist production.

In the conversation, Foucault remarks:

> One of the things that has preoccupied me for some time is the realization how difficult it is to kill oneself. ... Moreover, suicide is considered in the most negative way possible by society. Not only are we told that it's not good to kill ourselves but also that if someone commits suicide it's because things were going badly.[8]

Schroeter has in mind the idea of a sovereign suicide [Freitod][9] associated with extreme pleasure, with intensity: 'I don't understand how somebody very depressed would have the strength to commit suicide. I could kill myself only in a state of grace or extreme pleasure, but above all not in a state of depression.'[10] That extreme pleasure is an intensity, an intensity of life. Someone who is depressed does not possess the strength necessary for a sovereign suicide. His suicide [Suizid] would not express an affirmation of life. Rather, he is driven to it because life has become empty, meaningless and unbearable, because he is tired and exhausted, *because he can no longer produce, can no longer produce himself*. He commits suicide because of a rejection of life. It is not a voluntary death [Freitod], but a forced death, a death out of exhaustion. Such a death is possible only under neoliberal relations of production.

In his conversation with Schroeter, Foucault even ascribes to suicide the status of an act of cultural resistance: 'I am a partisan of a true cultural combat for reinstructing people that there is no conduct more beautiful, that merits more reflection with as much attention, than suicide. One should work on one's suicide all one's life.'[11] Foucault takes suicide to be an act of freedom. It is a sign of sovereignty to risk one's life, that is, *to turn life into a game*.

Following Foucault, we may define the art of life as a practice of suicide, of giving *oneself* death, of *de-psychologizing oneself*, of *playing*: 'The art of living is to eliminate psychology, to create, with oneself and others, individualities, beings, relations, unnameable qualities. If one fails to do that in one's life it isn't worth living.'[12] The art of life opposes the terror of psychology. We are today held captive by our psychology. The narcissistic retreat into the ego, into psychology, destroys the spaces of play, the *fantasy of play*. The art of life means escaping *oneself* in the *search for as yet unnamed forms of life and play*.

Today, to live means merely to produce. Everything moves from the sphere of play to that of production. We are all workers, and no longer players. Play itself is watered down; it becomes a leisure-time activity. Only weak play is tolerated, and it forms a functional element within production. The sacred seriousness of play has entirely given way to the profane seriousness of work and production. Life subordinated to the dictates of health, optimization and performance comes to resemble mere survival. It lacks splendour, sovereignty, intensity. The Roman satirist Juvenal expressed this well when he spoke of 'losing the reasons to live for the sake of staying alive' (*propter vitam vivendi perdere causas*).[13]

6

The End of History

In modernity the significance of work increases markedly while play is regarded with ever more suspicion. This is also reflected in philosophy. Hegel's dialectic of master and slave begins with a duel. The one who is determined to win will be the master. He wants to shine. He lives for the honour and glory of victory, and for that he is prepared to risk death. He puts his life at stake. As a player he does not shy away from the highest stake. The other one, by contrast, avoids battle out of fear of death. He wants not to win but to survive. He prefers survival to the glory of victory, of sovereignty. Thus, he does not risk death. He subordinates himself to the master and works for him as a slave. He decides in favour of work, of survival, and against the play of life and death. The master is a free man because he is prepared to stake his own life. He is a strong player, while the other is a worker, a slave.

Hegel does not side with the master but with the slave. He does so because he is a philosopher of modernity. Work, for him, has primacy. Thinking itself is work. Spirit works. Work forms the spirit. Hegel's dialectic of master and slave looks at human existence exclusively from the perspective of work. Hegel has no access to the freedom of the player who despises work and leaves it to the slave.

Following Hegel, Marx also holds on to the primacy of work. History begins with work: 'The first historical act of these individuals by which they differ from the animals is not that they think but that they begin to produce the means by which they live.'[1] Humans have a history because they work. Marx declares work to be the fundamental concept of Hegel's *Phenomenology of Spirit*:

> The importance of Hegel's *Phenomenology* and its final result – the dialectic of negativity as the moving and producing principle – lies in the fact that Hegel . . . grasps the nature of *labour* and conceives objective man – true, because real man – as the result of his *own labour*. . . . Hegel adopts the standpoint of modern political economy. He sees *labour* as the *essence*, the self-confirming essence, of man; . . .[2]

Given the primacy of work in Marx, it is noteworthy that his son-in-law, Paul Lafargue, wrote a tract entitled *The Right to Be Lazy*.[3] Lafargue begins by invoking the free man of ancient Greece:

> The Greeks in their era of greatness had only contempt for work: their slaves alone were permitted to labor: the free man knew only exercises for the body and mind.

... The philosophers of antiquity taught contempt for work, that degradation of the free man, the poets sang of idleness, that gift from the Gods: *O Melibae Deus nobis haec otia fecit* [Oh Melibaeus! A god has granted us this idleness; D.S.].[4]

Lafargue demands that the 'Rights of Man concocted by the metaphysical lawyers of the bourgeois revolution' be replaced with the 'Rights of Laziness'.[5] The realm of laziness, entirely free of the seriousness of work, devotes itself to beautiful play. Lafargue's pamphlet ends with the exclamation: 'O Laziness, have pity on our long misery! O Laziness, mother of the arts and noble virtues, be thou the balm of human anguish!'[6]

Kojève, in his interpretation of the dialectic of master and slave, also elevates work to the status of the motor of history: 'This creative education of Man by work (*Bildung*) creates History – i.e., human Time. Work is Time.'[7] Work forms the spirit and moves history forwards. It is the only agent of a history understood in terms of progress. Thus, the worker becomes the sole subject of history.

The end of work means the end of history. According to Kojève's initial idea of the 'post-historical', the 'American way of life' anticipates 'the "eternal present" future of all of humanity'.[8] The post-historical is characterized by 'Man's return to animality':[9]

In point of fact, the end of human Time or History – that is, the definitive annihilation of Man properly so-called or of the free and historical Individual – means quite simply the cessation of Action in the full sense of

58

the term. Practically, this means: the disappearance of wars and bloody revolutions. And also the disappearance of Philosophy; for since Man himself no longer changes essentially, there is no longer any reason to change the (true) principles which are at the basis of his understanding of the World and of himself. But all the rest can be preserved indefinitely; art, love, play, etc., etc.; in short, everything that makes Man *happy*.[10]

After travelling to Japan, Kojève formed an altogether different picture of the end of history, one located in a Japan that is thoroughly ritualized and strictly opposed to the American way of life. Here, humans lead not an animalistic life but a ritual one. To Kojève, Japan now appears as the *coming realm of ritual*: 'Instead of risking their lives in battle, they [i.e. the Japanese] have suspended it in the ceremonial – everyone was "in a position to live according to totally formalized values – that is, values completely empty of all 'human' content in the 'historical' sense."'[11] Post-historical society is characterized by a 'ruthless aesthetization', an aesthetic formalization, of life. It is inspired, Nietzsche would say, not by a will to truth but by a will to semblance, to play. It plays on surfaces and succumbs to the seduction of semblance [Schein]: 'Where historical man spoke of true and false, Nietzsche sees only "levels of appearance [Stufen der Scheinbarkeit] and, as it were, lighter and darker shades and tones of appearance – different *valeurs*."'[12] Japan foreshadows that *coming ritual society*, a society which can do without truth, without transcendence – a thoroughly aestheticized society in which *beautiful semblance* [der *schöne Schein*] will have taken the place of religion.

7

The Empire of Signs

Because of the compulsion of work and production, we are losing the capacity to *play*. We only rarely make playful use of language; we only put it to *work*. It is obliged to communicate information or produce meaning. As a result, we have no access to forms of language that shine all by themselves. Language as a medium of information has no splendour. It does not seduce. Poems are structures with strict forms that shine all by themselves. Very often, they do not communicate a message. They are characterized by an *excess of the signifier*; they are *luxurious*. We enjoy in particular their perfection of form. In poetry, language *plays*. For this reason, we hardly read poems any more. Poems are *magic ceremonies of language*. The *poetic principle* returns pleasure to language through a radical break with the economy of the production of meaning. The poetic does not produce. This is why '[t]he poetic is the insurrection of language against its own laws', against the laws that serve the purpose of producing meaning.[1] In poems we enjoy language itself. The working language of information, by contrast, cannot be enjoyed. The principle of work is opposed to the principle of pleasure.

Kant calls wit [den Witz] an 'intellectual luxury'.[2] In the case of wit, language succumbs to play. Thus, wit is 'blooming', just as 'nature seems to be carrying on more of a game with its flowers but a business with fruits'.[3] A witticism [der Witz] is not an utterance that may be reduced to an unambiguous meaning. It is a luxury, that is, it luxates, deviates, from the 'business' of meaning production. It is a linguistic form in which meaning, the signified, is not all that important. While language's intelligence consists of the production of meaning, in the case of witticisms language plays dumb, so to speak:

> Wit presents language with an opportunity to play dumber than it actually is, to evade its own dialectic and chains of meanings, in order to throw itself into a process of delirious contiguity . . . Wit demonstrates that language has an orientation toward non-meaning – provided it is enchained by its own play.[4]

In the case of witticisms, the effect emanates more from the signifier than the signified. Thus, they are difficult to paraphrase. Delirious contiguity is the poetic principle of wit. The signifiers licentiously enter into neighbourly relations without giving any consideration to the signified.

If the sign, the signifier, is completely absorbed by meaning, by the signified, then language loses all its magic and splendour. It becomes purely informational; it *works* instead of plays. Eloquence and linguistic elegance also derive from the luxury of the signifier. Only through the overabundance, the excess, of the signifier does language appear magical, poetic and seductive:

> This overabundant order of the signifier is that of magic (and poetry). . . . The long *work* of joining signifier and signified, the *work* of reason, somehow brakes and absorbs this fatal profusion. The magical seduction of the word must be reduced, annulled. And it will be so the day when all signifiers receive their signifieds, when all has become meaning and reality.[5]

What is mysterious is not the signified but the signifier without the signified. Magic spells do not convey any meaning. They are empty signs, so to speak. That is why they appear magical, like doors that lead nowhere.

Ritual signs cannot be assigned a determinate meaning either. Thus, they appear enigmatic. As language becomes increasingly functional and informational, the overabundance, the excess, of the signifier diminishes. Language is disenchanted. Pure information is nothing magical. It does not seduce. Language develops its magnificence, its seductive power, only thanks to the overabundance of the signifier. The culture of information has lost the magic that comes from the empty signifier. We now live in a *culture of the signified*, which dismisses the signifier, form, as something external. Our culture is hostile to pleasure and form.

Ritual is also characterized by an overabundance of the signifier. Thus, Roland Barthes idealizes Japan, a thoroughly ritualized country, as an empire of signs, a ceremonial empire of signifiers. The haiku poetic form, for instance, is determined by the overabundance of the signifier. Haikus pay little attention to the signified. They do not communicate anything. They are a pure play with language, with signifiers, that produces no meaning. Haikus are linguistic ceremonies:

> In the haiku, the limitation of language is the object of a concern which is inconceivable to us, for it is not a question of being concise (i.e., shortening the signifier without diminishing the density of the signified) but on the contrary of acting on the very root of meaning, so that this meaning will not melt, run, internalize, become implicit, disconnect, divagate . . . the haiku is not a rich thought reduced to a brief form, but a brief event which immediately finds its proper form.[6]

A haiku is subject to strict rules of play, and thus it cannot really be translated into another language. Forms which are proper to the Japanese language resist any kind of translation.

old pond
a frog jumps into
the sound of water[7]

The intense formalism and aestheticism that characterizes rituals in general also dominates everyday ritual practices in Japan. Take packaging, for instance. The Japanese put any trivial thing into a magnificent envelope. According to Barthes, the idea behind a Japanese parcel is 'that the triviality of the thing be disproportionate to the luxury of the envelope'.[8] In semiotic terms: the signifier (envelope) is more important than what it signifies, namely the signified, the content. The magnificent signifier delays the revelation of the possibly insignificant signified to a later time. It shines for itself, independently of the truth, the thing, it contains: 'what the Japanese carry, with a formicant energy, are actually empty signs'.[9] *The liturgy of emptiness dispels the capitalist economy of the commodity.* The Japanese parcel does not reveal anything. It distracts us from the thing and, in the first instance, presents the magnificent envelope. Thus, the Japanese parcel is opposed to the *commodity*, for which the packaging is something purely external, something that only exists in order to be quickly removed again. In a similar way, the kimono veils the body with an overabundance of signifiers, a play of colour and form. The body as a bearer of signifiers is opposed to the pornographic body, which is unveiled, and hence obscene. The pornographic body, free of signifiers, indicates only the naked signified, the naked truth, namely the sexual organ [das Geschlecht].

A Japanese tea ceremony subjects us to a minutely detailed process of ritualized gesture. Here, there is no space for psychology. Participants are truly [regelrecht] de-psychologized.[10] The proper movements of the hands and body have a *graphic clarity*, and there is no uncertainty about them deriving from the influence of the mind or soul. The actors immerse *themselves* in ritual gestures, and these gestures create an *absence*, a *forgetfulness of self*. In a tea ceremony, there is no communication. Nothing is communicated. There is ritual silence [Schweigen]. Ritual gesture takes the place of communication. *The soul falls silent.* In the stillness, participants exchange gestures which generate an intense being-with. The soothing effect of a tea ceremony results from the fact that its ritual silence is so strongly opposed to today's communicative noise, today's communication without community. The ceremony brings forth a community without communication.

For Barthes, the Japanese eye is not a place filled with soul. It is empty. Barthes is suspicious of the Western mythology of the soul: 'The Western eye is subject to a whole mythology of the soul, central and secret, whose fire, sheltered in the orbital cavity, radiates toward a fleshy, sensuous, passionate exterior.'[11] The Japanese eye is flat, without depth. The pupils are not dramatized by the deep cavity of the eye. Hegel, who does subscribe to the Western mythology of the soul, says that 'the bones of the eye-socket' should be emphasized such that 'the strengthened shadow in the orbits gives us of itself a feeling of depth and undistracted inner life'. The depth of the soul is emphasized by 'the sharply cut outline of the orbits'. Thus, the eye 'should not protrude or, as it were, project itself into the external world'.[12] What might Hegel have said about those *flat* eyes of the Far East that appear more like a fleeting stroke of the brush on the face, rather than being deeply set back in the orbital bones?

The empire of signs also dispenses with the *moral signified*. It is dominated not by *law* but by *rules*, by signifiers without the signified. Ritual society is a society of rules. It is based not on virtues or conscience but on a *passion for rules*. Unlike the moral law, rules are not *internalized*. They are simply *obeyed*. Morality presupposes a soul, and a person who *works* on its perfection. The more a person advances on the path of morality, the more self-respect she is due. Such narcissistic inwardness is wholly absent from the *ethics of politeness*.

Rules rest on agreement. They are formed through immanent sequences of signs, and therefore do not possess deep truth or transcendence. Rules do not have a metaphysical or theological foundation. The law, by contrast, presupposes a transcendent authority, such as God, that compels and prohibits. The pleasure derived from obeying a rule differs from the pleasure one takes in obeying or violating a law. The former is owed to a passion for play and for rules:

> In order to understand the intensity of ritual forms, one must rid oneself of the idea that all happiness derives from nature, and all pleasure from the satisfaction of a desire. On the contrary, games, the sphere of play, reveal a passion for rules, a giddiness born of rules, and a force that comes from ceremony, and not desire.[13]

Capitalism is based on the economy of desire. Thus, it is incompatible with a ritual society. The intensity of the ritual form arises out of a passion for rules, which creates an altogether different form of pleasure.

Politeness is pure form. Nothing is *intended* by it. It is empty. As a ritual form, it is devoid of any moral content. It is a sign, a signifier, that differs radically from 'politeness of the heart', which suggests a moral signified:

> Today we place the moral law above signs. The play of conventional forms is deemed hypocritical and immoral: we oppose it with 'the politeness of the heart' or even the radical impoliteness of desire. . . . It's true that eti-

66

quette and politeness (and ceremony in general) are no longer what they once were.[14]

As a form of ritual, politeness is without heart and without desire, without wish. It is more *art* than morality. It exhausts itself in the pure exchange of ritual gestures. Within the topology of Japanese politeness as a ritual form, there is no inside, no heart, that would render the politeness a merely external etiquette. It cannot be described using the opposition of inside and outside. It does not dwell in an outside that, as pure semblance, could be juxtaposed with the inside. Rather, one is *fully form, fully outside*:

> in order to give a present, I bow down, virtually to the level of the floor, and to answer me, my partner does the same: one and the same low line, that of the ground, joins the giver, the recipient, and the stake of the protocol, a box which may well contain nothing – or virtually nothing.[15]

A 'graphic form . . . is thereby given to the act of exchange, in which, by this form, is erased any greediness (the gift remains suspended between two disappearances)'.[16] The present, as a signifier without signified, is *pure mediation*, a *pure gift*.

> The gift is alone:
> it is touched
> neither by generosity
> nor by gratitude,
> the soul does not contaminate it[17]

In the empire of signs, the soul, psychology, is erased. There is no soul to infect the holy seriousness of ritual play. The place of psychology is taken by a *passion for rules*, a *passion of form*. This empire of signs is opposed to today's *empire of souls* who expose themselves and constantly produce themselves. The ceremonial empire of signs makes it possible to conceive of another form of life, another society, which would be free of narcissism because, in it, the ego [das Ich] would immerse *itself* in the ritual play of signs. The passion for rules de-internalizes the self.

Contemporary society is characterized by constant and relentless moralizing. But at the same time society is becoming more and more brutal. Forms of politeness are disappearing, disregarded by the cult of authenticity. Beautiful forms of conduct are becoming ever rarer. In this respect, too, we are becoming hostile towards form. Apparently, the ascendancy of morality is compatible with the barbarization of society. Morality is formless. Moral inwardness dispenses with form. One might even say: *the more moralizing a society, the more impolite it is*. Against this formless morality, we must defend an *ethics of beautiful forms*.

8

From Duelling to Drone Wars

In his treatise *Homo Ludens*, Huizinga emphasizes the playful character of war in archaic cultures. The strict rules to which war was subject in these societies made war akin to play. Huizinga does not deny that there was also extreme violence and brutal murder in the ancient world, but he positions war in the sacral sphere of play:

> A solemn compact in which the rules were laid down was deposited beforehand in the temple of Artemis. The time and place for the encounter were therein appointed. All missiles were forbidden: spears, arrows, slingstones; only the sword and the lance were allowed.[1]

The prohibition of certain weapons and the agreement on the time and place of battle underline the play-like character of war in the ancient world. The 'battle-ground is marked out with wooden pegs or hazel switches'.[2] There is a level battlefield to ensure an even contest between the belligerents.

Huizinga remarks that the ritualization of war 'certainly raised the tone', that is, improved ethical standards.[3] The 'exchanging of civilities with the enemy' that is characteristic of ritual combat presupposes the explicit acknowledgement of the other party as an equal opponent. The belligerents honour one another in all sorts of ways, exchanging weapons as presents, for instance. Rituals generally have a strong formative power. Warfare as ritual combat harnesses violence by imposing a form, strict rules of play, on its use. Violence gives way to the passion of play.

Duelling is also a form of ritual combat, deriving from the ancient practice of trial by combat. There is a sacral dimension inherent in the duel. The outcome resembles a divine judgement: *dike* (Greek: right) and *tyche* (Greek: fate, accident, divine providence) blend into each other. As a form of trial by combat, the duel of early modern times was also subject to specific legal rules. Before the duel, there were first proceedings at a so-called court of honour, which did not differ significantly from civil court proceedings. As a form of ritual combat, the duel was subject to strict rules of play. Symmetry between the duellers was meticulously ensured. The duel took the form of ritual play: 'The spot where the duel is fought bears all the marks of a play-ground; the weapons have to be exactly alike as in certain games; there is a signal for the start and the finish, and the number of shots is prescribed.'[4] Anyone who refused to take part in a duel when challenged was considered to have dishonoured himself, and was demoted from his rank. In such ritual combat what is at stake is not the destruction of the opponent but honour itself. The duellers proved their honour, their 'manly honour', by facing the fight and risking their lives. Regardless of the outcome, a duel restored the duellers' honour. After it, society adjudged them men of honour.

According to the chivalric code, which had a decisive influence on the development of the notion of military honour in Europe, it is not honourable to attack an enemy without putting yourself at risk. It is only honourable to attack the enemy on the battlefield. It is dishonourable, by contrast, to kill the enemy in an underhanded way – by poisoning, for instance. Symmetry and reciprocity must be ensured. Of particular importance when it comes to the fairness of war as ritual combat is the symmetry of means of battle. If one's enemy only possesses a sword, then one cannot use a crossbow. Throughout the history of warfare, there were repeated attempts at limiting the use of lethal weapons. As Carl Schmitt would put it, these attempts served the purpose of 'hedging war'.[5]

In his treatise *On War*, Clausewitz defines war as ritual combat: 'I shall not begin by expounding a pedantic, literary definition of war, but go straight to the heart of the matter, to the duel. War is nothing but a duel on a larger scale.'[6] War is an orderly, rule-guided duel. According to Clausewitz's famous formulation, it is the 'continuation of political intercourse, carried on with other means'.[7] The emphasis here is not, as is generally assumed, on 'other means' – that is, on violence – but on the political. As war is a way of pursuing political ends, it is possible to return to a politics without violence after war has ended. The rules of the game to which all belligerents commit themselves ensure that, after the war is over, there is space left for politics. By contrast, killing without rules, pure violence, destroys the political space. War as large-scale duelling differs fundamentally from the kind of military action we see today, which is increasingly degenerating into ruthless killing.

Modern wars lack the character of play. Here, too, the basic formula applies: *the compulsion of production destroys play*. Modern wars are *battles of production*. They are therefore not led by sovereign players but by soldiers who are labouring slaves: 'Therefore the impotence of modern wars of which I spoke: the pathological excess of riches that cannot be endlessly accumulated is expended by slaves who are afraid of death and cannot play, except in a wretched way.'[8] Walter Benjamin also derives the logic of modern war from the destructive logic of production:

> if the natural use of productive forces is impeded by the property system, then the increase in technological means, in speed, in sources of energy will press toward an unnatural use. This is found in war ... The most horrifying features of imperialist war are determined by the discrepancy between the enormous means of production and their inadequate use in the process of production (in other words, by unemployment and the lack of markets).[9]

Marshall McLuhan's thesis, 'the medium is the message', also applies to weapons as media. A medium is not merely the bearer of a message; rather, the message is produced by the medium itself. A medium is not a neutral container carrying different contents. Rather, a new medium creates a specific content, for instance a new perception. The deployment of a radically different medium of destruction is therefore not simply a technological issue: rather, it changes the character of war itself. Schmitt ruminates on the deployment of fighter planes, for instance, which seem to make war as a duel impossible.

The head-to-head confrontation between warring parties reflects the fact that they are legally, even morally, of equal standing. The opponent is explicitly recognized as an enemy (*iustus hostis*). But the use of fighter planes does not permit any face-to-face confrontation. Superiority in the topological sense, that is, in the sense of being above the enemy, generates a different mental attitude towards the enemy. The asymmetry in the means of destruction at each party's disposal leads the superior one to adopt an altogether different estimation of the enemy. The enemy is degraded into the criminal: 'The superior force considers its superiority in weaponry to be proof of its *iusta causa* and declares the enemy to be a criminal, because it is no longer possible to realize the concept of *iustus hostis*.'[10] Hence, the medium is the message. Technological superiority turns into moral superiority. Technology and ethics condition each other.

An enemy in a war is not a criminal who must be destroyed at any cost. Rather, he is an equal opponent, a competing player. Such an enemy is afforded equal rights. With drone warfare, we reach the pinnacle of asymmetry. The degradation and transformation of the opponent into a criminal is the precondition of targeted killing, which resembles a kind of policing. Drone warfare completely dispenses with the reciprocity, the reciprocal relationship, that constitutes war as ritual combat. The attacker is wholly invisible. A screen is not an opponent.

Killing with the click of a mouse is a hunting of criminals that is more brutal than the hunting of game. A true hunt is not mindless killing: it is subject to strict rules. Rituals are performed before, during and after a chase. Between hunter and quarry there is a kind of reciprocity, a symmetry. The animal must be killed face-to-face. Before the killing it must be 'addressed'. An animal must never be killed while asleep. It is asked to wake up. It must also only be wounded in particular places. It is prohibited, for instance, to injure the animal's eyes, and it thus retains its gaze until the end. Even in the case of hunting, then, there is a reciprocal relationship. The other, after all, is the *gaze*.

The total asymmetry of drone warfare renders the concept of war obsolete. With regard to air war, Schmitt speaks of a 'violent measure' [Zwangsmaßnahme]: 'To war on both sides belongs a certain chance, a minimum of possibility for victory. Once that ceases to be the case, the opponent becomes nothing more than an object of violent measures.'[11] War as ritual combat is anything but the mere enforcement of such violent measures against the opponent. It is a game characterized by reciprocity. Drone warfare, as the enforcement of violent measures against the opponent, as the hunting of criminals, lacks any playful character. Here, death is *produced mechanically*. Drone pilots *work* shifts. For them, killing is mainly *work*. After they have performed their duty, they are ceremoniously handed a 'scorecard' that confirms how many people they have killed.[12] As in the case of any other work, what counts above all else is *performance* – even when it con-

74

cerns the killing of other humans. Algorithms facilitate the mechanical *production* of death. There is something pornographic, something obscene, about killing as a data-driven operation. The opponent is dissolved into data. As a former director of the US National Security Agency put it: 'We kill people based on metadata.'[13] The opponent who is to be destroyed is now no more than a set of data. Drone warfare is dataistic killing. The killing takes place without any fighting, is devoid of any drama, any fate. It is carried out mechanically, under the merciless guidance of data streams. The goal is *dataistically transparent killing*. Today, everything is made to fit the form of *production*. The form of war that produces death is diametrically opposed to war as ritual combat. Production and ritual are mutually exclusive. Drone warfare is an image of the society in which everything has become a matter of work, production and performance.

9

From Myth to Dataism

In the ancient world not only war but also the transfer of knowledge took the form of play. Sacral riddle-solving competitions were an essential part of sacrificial cults, as important as the sacrifice itself. They vivified and solidified myth as the foundational knowledge of a community. Huizinga suspects that the very beginnings of philosophy are to be found in ritual games of riddle-solving:

> The earliest philosophers speak in tones of prophecy and rapture. Their sublime self-assurance is that of the sacrificial priest or mystagogue. Their problems deal with the *fons et origo* of things, with ἀρχή – the Beginning, and φύσις – Nature . . . It is always the same old cosmogonic teasers, propounded since time immemorial in riddle-form and solved in myth.[1]

Early Greek philosophy displays an agonistic character. It is all game and competition:

> we can say with certainty that the philosopher, from the earliest times to the late Sophists and Rhetors, always appeared as a typical champion. He challenged his rivals, he attacked them with vehement criticism and extolled his own opinions as the only true ones with all the boyish cocksureness of archaic man. In style and form the earliest samples of philosophy are polemical and agonistic. They invariably speak in the first person singular. When Zeno of Elea attacks his adversaries he does it with aporias – that is, he starts ostensibly from their premises only to arrive at two contradictory and mutually exclusive conclusions. The form points as clearly as anything can to the riddle. Zeno asks: 'If space is something, what can it be in?' For Heraclitus, the 'dark philosopher', nature and life are a *griphos*, an enigma, and he himself is the riddle-solver.[2]

The sophists stage an art of argument, a play of astuteness, the point of which is to snare one's opponent. The term 'problem', from the Greek *problemata*, originally meant the question presented to the opponent for a solution. 'Solving', in this context, should be taken literally. It means to free oneself from ropes and snares. The agonistic character of philosophy represents the cosmic process, understood as the eternal strife between primordial oppositions. For Heraclitus, war is father of all, and according to Empedocles, affection (Greek: *philia*) and strife (Greek: *neikos*) are the two fundamental principles that determine the course of the world.

The Platonic dialogues still exhibit elements of play. The *Symposium* is structured like a ritual competition: the participants in the conversation compete with speeches praising the god Eros. Plato speaks of a judge:

> 'Now you've gone *too* far, Socrates,' Agathon replied. 'Well, eat your dinner. Dionysus will soon enough be the judge of our claims to wisdom!' Socrates took his seat after that and had his meal, according to Aristodemus. When dinner was over, they poured a libation to the god, sang a hymn, and – in short – followed the whole ritual. Then they turned their attention to drinking.[3]

In the *Gorgias*, Socrates and Callicles behave more like two duellers than like two engaged in a dialogue; it is more confrontation than discussion. It resembles a dramatic form of ritual combat. Indeed, between two incompatible positions on power and justice no mediation is possible: it is only a question of winning or losing. The agonistic character of the dialogue is plain:

> And what becomes clear to any reader of the text is not that one interlocutor will convince the other, but that there will be a victor and a vanquished. This is after all what explains why Socrates's methods in this dialogue are hardly fairer than those of Callicles. Wanting the ends means wanting the means, and it is a matter of winning, especially of winning in the eyes of young men who witness the scene.[4]

Plato's dialogues are theatrical, and the 'joys of the theatre' determine the course of the game.[5]

Despite the obvious elements of play in his dialogues, Plato inaugurates the transition from myth to truth. In the name of truth, he distances himself from the play to which the sophists are devoted. Plato's Socrates accuses them of lacking seriousness:

> These things are the frivolous part of study (which is why I also tell you that the men are jesting); and I call these things 'frivolity' because even if a man were to learn many or even all such things, he would be none the wiser as to how matters stand but would only be able to make fun of people, tripping them up and overturning them by means of the distinctions in words, just like the people who pull the chair out from under a man who is going to sit down and then laugh gleefully when they see him sprawling on his back.[6]

The sophists are seen as mere travelling showmen who are occupied solely with the playful. But play has now to give way to the work of uncovering the truth.

Huizinga is probably to be credited with having taught us about the playful character of human action in archaic cultures. But he turns play into something absolute, and he therefore misses the decisive paradigm shift within knowledge transfer in the history of the Occident, namely the transition from myth to truth, which coincides with the transition from play to work. Along the path towards work, thinking gradually distances itself from its origin in play.

The mistrust of play intensifies in the age of the Enlightenment. Kant subordinates play to work. His aesthetics, for instance, is characterized by the primacy of work. In the face of beauty, the cognitive faculties, namely imagination and understanding, are in play mode. The subject likes what is beautiful; the beautiful creates a feeling of pleasure by triggering a harmonious interplay of the cognitive faculties. The beautiful does not by itself produce knowledge, but it *entertains* the cognitive mechanisms and, by doing so, promotes the production of knowledge. Kant is deeply irritated by the idea of pure play as an end in itself. Music is to be avoided insofar as it is incapable of performing any thinking 'business', 'because it merely plays with sensations'.[7] Because music merely plays, it is incompatible with conceptual work. For Kant, the pictorial arts are to be preferred to music because they are compatible with the 'business' of thinking, that is, the production of knowledge. Unlike music, 'they set the imagination into a free play that is nevertheless also suitable for the understanding', and at the same time they 'conduct a business by bringing about a product that serves the concepts of the understanding as [a] . . . vehicle'.[8] In this passage, Kant speaks explicitly of a 'product' and, as he often does, of a 'business'. Limits must be set to the imagination's urge to play so that play can serve the purposes of the understanding, namely the production of knowledge. Play is subordinated to work and production.

The Enlightenment assumes the autonomy of the subject of knowledge. Kant's 'Copernican revolution' introduces this autonomy: it is not we who revolve around the things; the things must take their bearings from us.

This would be just like the first thoughts of Copernicus, who, when he did not make good progress in the expla-

80

nation of the celestial motions if he assumed that the entire celestial host revolves around the observer, tried to see if he might not have greater success if he made the observer revolve and left the stars at rest. Now in metaphysics we can try in a similar way regarding the **intuition** of objects. If intuition has to conform to the constitution of the objects, then I do not see how we can know anything of them a priori; but if the object (as an object of the senses) conforms to the constitution of our faculty of intuition, then I can very well represent this possibility to myself.[9]

Knowledge of the world is made possible by *a priori forms*, that is, forms that are given in advance of any experience and are inherent in the subject of knowledge. Kant's idealism rests on the belief that the human subject is the master of the production of knowledge. Kant's universe is centred around a free, autonomous subject as the institution that provides the forms and laws of knowledge.

Today, a further paradigm shift is silently taking place. The Copernican anthropological turn which made man an autonomous producer of knowledge is being superseded by the dataistic turn. The human being now has to comply with data. No longer the producer of knowledge, the human being cedes its sovereignty to data. Dataism puts an end to the idealism and humanism of the Enlightenment.[10] The human being is no longer the sovereign subject of knowledge, the originator of knowledge. *Knowledge is now produced mechanically*. The data-driven production of knowledge takes place without the involvement of the human subject or consciousness. Enormous volumes of data displace the human being from its central position as producer of knowledge, and the human being itself is reduced to a data set, a variable that can be calculated and manipulated.

The knowledge produced by big data escapes understanding. Human cognition is not powerful enough. Processors are faster than a human being precisely because they neither think nor understand; they only calculate. The proponents of dataism would argue that humans invented thinking because they cannot calculate fast enough, and that the age of thinking will prove to be a short historical interlude.

Transparency, the imperative of dataism, is the source of the compulsion to transform everything into data and information, that is, to make it visible. It is a *compulsion of production*. Transparency does not declare the human being to be free; it declares data and information free. It is an efficient form of domination in which total communication and total surveillance coincide. This form of domination presents itself as freedom. Big data produces a knowledge for domination that allows for the manipulation and direction of the human psyche. From this perspective, dataism's imperative of transparency represents not a continuation but the end of the Enlightenment.

The compulsion of production eliminates the space of games and narration. Algorithmic processes of calculation are not narrative but only additive, which is why they can always be accelerated. Thinking, by contrast, cannot be accelerated. Theories still contain elements of narrative. Algorithms count, but they do not recount. The transition from myth to dataism is the transition from recounting to pure counting. Dataism turns the production of knowledge into something pornographic.

Thinking is more erotic than calculating. It is Eros who gives wings to thinking: 'I call it Eros, the oldest of the gods according to Parmenides. . . . The beat of that god's wings moves me every time I take a substantial step in my thinking and venture onto untrodden paths.'[11] Without Eros, the steps of thinking degenerate into the steps of a calculation, that is, the steps of work to be performed. Calculation is naked, pornographic. Thinking dresses itself in figures. It is often squiggly. Calculations, by contrast, follow a linear path.

Thinking has the character of play. Under the compulsion of work and production, it becomes alienated from its essence: 'The kind of thinking that provided the foundation for work and compulsion is bankrupt. Having in the past assigned to work and to the useful the egregious role with which we are now all-too familiar, it is time that free thinking remembered that it is play to the core.'[12] Along the way from myth to dataism, thinking loses the element of play altogether. It comes close to calculation. But the steps in thinking are not the steps of a calculation which simply repeat the same operation over and over again. Rather, they are moves in a game, or dancing steps, which create something totally different, introduce an altogether different order among things:

> We are all players, gamblers. In other words, our most fervent hope is that rational sequences of events will unravel every now and again and be replaced, if only for a short time, by an unprecedented sequence of a different order, a wonderfully tumultuous course of events …[13]

10

From Seduction to Porn

Seduction does not depend on gender difference. In Kierkegaard's *The Seducer's Diary*, gender is altogether absent. The sexual act, which is not even explicitly mentioned in the book, plays a subordinate role within the drama of seduction. Seduction is a game. It belongs to the order of ritual. Sex, by contrast, is a function. It is part of the order of the natural. Seduction is structured like a ritual duel. Everything takes place in an 'almost liturgical realm of challenge and duel'.[1] Kierkegaard compares seduction to fencing:

> Be careful; such a glance from below is more dangerous than one that is *geradeaus* [direct]! It is like fencing; and what weapon is as sharp, as penetrating, as gleaming in its movement and thereby as illusive as the eye? You feint a high quarte, as the fencer says, and then

lunge instantaneously; the more swiftly the lunge can follow upon the feint, the better. It is an indescribable moment, the instant of the feint. The opponent feels, as it were, the cut; he is struck; and so he is, but in a place quite different from what he thought.[2]

Being a duel, seduction implies a playful use of power. In this context, we should distance ourselves from the common idea that power is suppression, something negative or evil. Power is not just repressive; it is also seductive, even erotic. The play with power is characterized by reciprocity. Thus, Foucault interprets power from the perspective of the economy of pleasure:

> Power is not evil. Power is games of strategy. We all know that power is not evil! For example, let us take sexual or amorous relationships: to wield power over the other in a sort of open-ended strategic game where the situation may be reversed is not evil; it's a part of love, of passion and sexual pleasure.[3]

Seduction requires a scenic, playful distance that leads me away from my personal psychology. The intimacy of love falls outside the sphere of seduction. It represents the end of play and the beginning of psychology and confession. It distrusts the playful scenes. Eroticism in the form of seduction is different from the intimacy of love, for in intimacy the playful aspect is lost. Seduction is based on *extimacy*, on the *exteriority of the other*, an exteriority that escapes the sphere of the intimate. Constitutive of seduction is a *fantasy of the other*.

Porn, finally, marks the end of seduction. Here, the

other is effaced altogether. Pornographic pleasure is narcissistic. It derives from the immediate consumption of an
object that is offered naked. Today, even souls, like genitals [das Geschlecht], are offered unveiled. The loss of
any capacity for illusion, semblance, theatre, play, drama
– that signals the triumph of pornography.

Porn is a phenomenon of transparency. The age of
pornography is the age of unambiguousness. Today, we
no longer have a sense for phenomena such as secrets or
riddles. Ambiguities or ambivalences cause us discom-
fort. Because of their ambiguity, jokes are also frowned
upon. Seduction requires the negativity of the secret. The
positivity of the unambiguous only allows for sequential
processes. Even reading is acquiring a pornographic form.
The pleasure of reading a text resembles that of watching
a striptease. It derives from a progressive unveiling of
truth as though it were a sexual organ [der Wahrheit als
Geschlecht]. We rarely read poems any more. Unlike
popular crime novels, they do not contain a final truth.
Poems play with fuzzy edges. They do not admit of pornographic reading; they do not possess pornographic
sharpness. They resist the *production of meaning*.

Political correctness also condemns ambiguity:
'So-called "politically correct" practices . . . request a
form of transparency and lack of ambiguity – so as to . . .
neutralize the traditional rhetorical and emotional halo
of seduction.'[4] Ambiguities are essential to the language
of eroticism. The rigorous linguistic hygiene of political correctness makes erotic seduction impossible. Today,
eroticism is stifled by political correctness as well as by
porn.

The compulsion of production and performance today

takes hold of all areas of life, including sexuality. To produce originally meant to present and make visible. In porn, the genitals [Geschlecht] are produced, presented, made totally visible. In today's pornography, not even ejaculation is hidden. It is also produced. The final result of the performance is not meant to remain concealed. The more there is of the product, the greater the producer's capacity to perform. He produces himself in front of the eyes of his female partner, who is the co-producer of the pornographic process. The sexual act in today's porn films seems mechanical. The principle of performance has also taken hold of sex, giving the body the function of a sexual machine. Sex, performance, achievement, libido and production come to be bound up with one another.[5] Baudrillard derives the compulsion to ejaculate from the compulsion of production:

> We remain perplexed and vaguely compassionate when confronted with cultures for which the sexual act is not a finality in itself, for which sexuality does not have the mortal seriousness of an energy to be liberated, of an ejaculation to be forced, a production at any price, or hygienic auditing of the body. Cultures that preserve lengthy procedures of enticement and sensuality, long series of gifts and counter-gifts, with sex being but one service amongst others, and the act of love one possible end-term to a prescribed, ritualistic interchange.[6]

Today, the time-consuming play of seduction is increasingly discarded in favour of the immediate gratification of desire. Seduction and production are not compatible: 'Ours is a culture of premature ejaculation.

Increasingly all seduction, all manner of enticement – which is always a highly ritualized process – is effaced behind a naturalized sexual imperative, behind the immediate and imperative realization of desire.[7] Playing is something altogether different from the gratification of desire. That libido which represents capital at the level of the body is hostile to play. Capital not only brings with it the labour power of the energetic body but also the sexual power of the libidinal body. Libido and drive are forms of production. They are opposed to the form of seduction.

Porn pervades the neoliberal dispositif as its general principle. Under the compulsion of production, everything is being presented, made visible, exposed and exhibited. Everything is subjected to the relentless light of transparency. Communication becomes pornographic when it becomes transparent, when it is smoothed out into an accelerated exchange of information. Language becomes pornographic once it no longer *plays*, once it only conveys information. The body becomes pornographic when it loses all its scenic aspects, when it is simply required to function. The pornographic body lacks any symbolism. The ritualized body, by contrast, is a splendid stage, with secrets and deities written into it. Sounds, too, become pornographic if they lose their subtlety and allusiveness, and are only there to produce affects and emotions. Digital tools for processing audio tracks include a setting called 'In your face', which gives sounds an impression of immediacy.[8] The sounds are, as it were, poured directly into the face: a *facial*.[9] Images that affect the eye and the genitals [das Geschlecht] immediately, before any hermeneutic process, are pornographic.

What is pornographic is the immediate contact, the *copulation*, of image and eye.

Today, we live in a post-sexual age. The excessive visibility, the pornographic *overproduction*, of sex puts an end to sex. Porn kills off sexuality and eroticism more effectively than moral repression ever could have hoped to. Lars von Trier's film *Nymphomaniac* heralds the post-sexual age. As one critic says of the film:

> The message might as well be: 'Forget about sex.' For at no point does the film show sexuality in a seductive way. It is pornographic because it forces the spectator to look closely and for long stretches of time at what is immediately presented. But what can be seen there is wrinkled, crooked, hairy, and greyish-yellow, in other words roughly as attractive as the sexual organ of any other mammal.[10]

In Latin, meat is *caro*. In the post-sexual age, pornography is so intensified as to become *carography*. What destroys sexuality is not the negativity of prohibition or deprivation but the *positivity of overproduction*. The pathology of today's society is the excess of positivity. It is a 'too much', not a 'too little', that is making us sick.

NOTES

Chapter 1 The Compulsion of Production

1 Gadamer, 'The Relevance of the Beautiful', in *The Relevance of the Beautiful and Other Essays*, p. 47.
2 Saint-Exupéry, *The Wisdom of the Sands*, p. 16.
3 Arendt, *The Human Condition*, p. 137.
4 Handke, *Phantasien der Wiederholung*, p. 8.
5 See 'Tee trinkend die Welt verändern? Yes, we Kännchen', at https://blog.naturkost.com/2016/11/charitea-bio-tee-fair-trade.
6 Douglas, *Natural Symbols*, p. 1.
7 Transl. note: See Türcke, *Hyperaktiv! Kritik der Aufmerksamkeitsdefizitkultur*.
8 Kierkegaard, *Repetition and Philosophical Crumbs*, p. 3.
9 Ibid.
10 Ibid., p. 4.
11 Handke, *Phantasien der Wiederholung*, p. 57.
12 Rosa, *Resonances*, p. 173.

13 Transl. note: 'Community' in English in the original.

14 Barthes, *The Neutral*, p. 124.

15 The need for ritual and fixed rules is being felt again following years of excessive deregulation. It is no coincidence that the subtitle of Jordan B. Peterson's well-known self-help book, *12 Rules for Life*, is *An Antidote to Chaos*. The demand for individually designed rites to mark the phases of life and their transitional points is also on the increase, with the place of priests now taken by so-called ritual designers. These novel rituals have to obey the imperative of authenticity and creativity. But they are not rituals in the proper sense. They do not exert the symbolic force which directs life towards something higher and thus provides meaning and orientation. Where there is no longer a higher order, rituals disappear.

Chapter 2 The Compulsion of Authenticity

1 Taylor, *The Ethics of Authenticity*, p. 29.

2 Ibid., pp. 40f.

3 Sennett, *The Fall of Public Man*, London: Penguin, 1974, p. 11.

4 Huizinga, *Homo Ludens*, p. 192. [Transl. note: The German text differs from the English. The first sentence runs: 'It can hardly be denied that a general tendency of culture to become more serious is a typical phenomenon of the nineteenth century.']

5 Sennett, *The Fall of Public Man*, p. 29.

6 Alain, *On Happiness*, p. 45, quoted in Robert Pfaller, *On the Pleasure Principle in Culture*, p. 231.

7 James, 'The Gospel of Relaxation', in *The Heart of William James*, p. 132.

8 Pfaller, *Das schmutzige Heilige und die reine Vernunft*, p. 129.

9 Ibid., p. 92.

Chapter 3 Rituals of Closure

1 Sennett, *The Fall of Public Man*, p. 335. [Transl. note: The English and German versions of the last sentence differ significantly. The German has: 'Die Stetigkeit des Selbst, die Unabgeschlossenheit und Unabschließbarkeit seiner Regungen sind ein wesentlicher Zug des Narzissmus' (Sennett, *Verfall und Ende des öffentlichen Lebens*, p. 581), which translates as: 'The continuity of the self, the incompleteness and impossibility of the closure of its impulses, is an essential trait of narcissism.' The corresponding English passage in full is: 'The self is real only if it is continuous; it is continuous only if one practices continual self-denial. When closure does occur, experience seems detached from the self, and so the person seems threatened with a loss. Thus the quality of a narcissistic impulse is that it must be a continual subjective state.']

2 Transl. note: For Han's use of 'de-siting' and 'off-sites', terms that originate in Martin Heidegger and Carl Schmitt, see Han, *What is Power?*, pp. 80–3.

3 Nádas, *Behutsame Ortsbestimmung*, p. 5. [Transl. note: The German book contains two texts, 'Genaue Ortsbestimmung' and 'Der eigene Tod', originally published separately in Hungarian: 'A helyzsin óvatos meghározása' (A careful definition of a place), in: *Hátországi napló: Újabb usszék* (Diary from the hinterland: recent essays), Pécs: Jelenkor, 2006, and *Saját halál* (One's own death), Pécs: Jelenkor, 2004].

4 Ibid., p. 16.

5 Ibid., p. 11.

6 Ibid., p. 25.

7 Transl. note: 'Mapping' in English in the original.

8 Ibid., p. 8.

9 Ibid., p. 17.

10 Ibid., p. 33.

11 Ibid., p. 78.

12 Hegel, *Lectures on the Philosophy of History*, p. 237.

13 Ibid., p. 235.

14 Cf. Bauman, *Retrotopia*.

15 Cf. Han, *Hyperkulturalität, Kultur und Globalisierung*.

16 Deleuze and Guattari, *A Thousand Plateaus*, p. 26.

17 Gadamer, 'The Relevance of the Beautiful', p. 42.

Chapter 4 Festivals and Religion

1 Quoted after Agamben, *Nudities*, p. 110.

2 Rosenzweig, *The Star of Redemption*, p. 334.

3 Ibid., p. 332.

4 Ibid., p. 333.

5 Ibid.

6 Ibid., pp. 327f.

7 Agamben and Ferrando, *The Unspeakable Girl*, p. 10.

8 Transl. note: The German 'Ruhe' means 'silence' as well as 'rest', 'absence of movement', 'calmness', 'relaxation'. From this point, the intended meaning of 'Ruhe' shifts from that of silence to that of rest.

9 Kerény, *Antike Religion*, p. 47.

10 Durkheim, *The Elementary Forms of the Religious Life*, p. 307.

11 Ibid., pp. 349f.

12 Transl. note: The current inflationary use of 'to celebrate' in the Anglophone world nicely illustrates Han's point; within the paradigm of compulsive production, everything, hence nothing, may be celebrated. The following sentence plays on 'Begehung', meaning an 'on-site inspection', a walk around an area.

13 Transl. note: 'Hochzeit' means 'wedding'.

14 Gadamer, 'The Relevance of the Beautiful', p. 45.

15 Ibid., p. 53.

16 Transl. note: 'Event management' and, below, 'event' are in English in the original.

17 Transl. note: 'Leisure sickness' in English in the original.

18 Agamben, *Profanations*, p. 84.

19 Heidegger, 'Language in the Poem: A Discussion on Georg Trakl's Poetic Work', in *On the Way to Language*, pp. 159f.

Chapter 5 *A Game of Life and Death*

1 Bataille, *Die Aufhebung der Ökonomie*, p. 312.

2 Frazer, *The Golden Bough*, pp. 276f.

3 Bataille, *Die Aufhebung der Ökonomie*, p. 326.

4 Baudrillard, *Symbolic Exchange and Death*, pp. 130f [translation modified].

5 Ibid., p. 147.

6 *Tageszeitung*, 2 April 2009.

7 Foucault, 'Passion According to Werner Schroeter', in *Foucault Live*, p. 317.

8 Ibid., pp. 317f.

9 Transl. note: German has several expressions for suicide: 'Freitod', 'Selbstmord' and 'Suizid'. 'Freitod' stresses the voluntary nature of the act; 'Suizid' belongs to the clinical register. Up to this point, Han has used the term 'Selbstmord'.

10 Ibid., p. 318.

11 Ibid.

12 Ibid., p. 317.

13 Quoted after Bataille, *Die Aufhebung der Ökonomie*, p. 326.

Chapter 6 *The End of History*

1 Marx, *Die Deutsche Ideologie*, MEW, vol. 3, p. 20 (footnote). [Transl. note: The sentence was crossed out by Marx in the manuscript. It is given in a footnote to the German edition, but omitted in the English edition.]

2 Marx, 'Economic and Philosophical Manuscripts (1844)', in *Early Writings*, pp. 385f.

3 Transl. note: The original French title continues 'Refutation of the "Right to Work" of 1848'.

4 Lafargue, *The Right to Be Lazy*, p. 12.

5 Ibid., p. 29.

6 Ibid., p. 57.

7 Kojève, *Introduction to the Reading of Hegel*, p. 53.

8 Ibid., p. 161 (footnote).

9 Ibid., p. 160 (footnote).

10 Ibid., p. 159 (footnote).

11 Kojève, *Überlebensformen*, p. 49. [Transl. note: The quotation is taken from Jacob Taubes, 'Ästhetisierung der Wahrheit im Posthistoire', which forms part of *Überlebensformen*. The quotation within the quotation is from Kojève, *Introduction to the Reading of Hegel*, p. 162 (footnote)].

12 Ibid., p. 54. [Transl. note: The quotation is from Taubes, 'Ästhetisierung'. Taubes quotes from Nietzsche, *Beyond Good and Evil*, §34, p. 35].

Chapter 7 *The Empire of Signs*

1 Baudrillard, *Symbolic Exchange and Death*, p. 198.

2 Transl. note: The German term 'Witz' may mean 'wit' or 'joke'.

3 Kant, *Anthropology from a Pragmatic Point of View*, p. 95.

4 Baudrillard, *Das Andere selbst*, p. 66.

5 Baudrillard, *Fatal Strategies*, p. 186 (my emphasis, B.-C. H.).

6 Barthes, *Empire of Signs*, p. 75.

7 Basho, *The Complete Haiku*, p. 59.

8 Barthes, *Empire of Signs*, p. 46.

9 Ibid.

10 Transl. note: There is some wordplay in the German here. The expression 'regelrecht' literally translates as 'according to a rule', so the text is suggesting that there is a rule-bound method of de-psychologizing being followed in the ceremony.

11 Ibid., p. 102.

12 Hegel, *Aesthetics: Lectures on Fine Art*, p. 734.

13 Baudrillard, *Seduction*, p. 132.

14 Baudrillard, *Fatal Strategies*, p. 209.

15 Barthes, *Empire of Signs*, pp. 65 ff.

16 Ibid., p. 68.

17 Ibid., p. 67.

Chapter 8 From Duelling to Drone Wars

1 Huizinga, *Homo Ludens*, p. 96.

2 Ibid., p. 99.

3 Ibid., p. 103.

4 Ibid., p. 95.

5 Transl. note: See Schmitt, *The Nomos of the Earth*, pp. 43–4, where Schmitt's expression 'Hegung' is variously translated as 'enclosure' or as the 'bracketing' of war. The German term's polysemy is probably best conveyed by 'hedging', also frequently found in the Schmitt literature.

6 Clausewitz, *On War*, p. 83.

7 Ibid., p. 99.

8 Bataille, *Die Aufhebung der Ökonomie*, p. 333.

9 Benjamin, 'The Work of Art in the Age of Its Technological Reproducibility: Second Version', in *The Work of Art in the Age of Its Technological Reproducibility: Second Version and Other Writings*, p. 42.

10 Schmitt, *The Nomos of the Earth*, p. 321 [translation modified].

11 Ibid., p. 320.

12 Transl. note: 'Scorecard' in English in the original.

13 Transl. note: See, e.g., https://abcnews.go.com/blogs/headlines/2014/05/ex-nsa-chief-we-kill-people-based-on-metadata and https://www.youtube.com/watch?v=UdQiz0Vavmc, showing the former Director of the NSA, General Michael Hayden, making the remark.

Chapter 9 From Myth to Dataism

1 Huizinga, *Homo Ludens*, p. 116.
2 Ibid., pp. 115f.
3 Plato, *Symposium*, in *Complete Works*, 175e-176a, p. 461.
4 Badiou, 'Thinking the Event', in Badiou and Žižek, *Philosophy in the Present*, p. 4.
5 Ibid., p. 5.
6 Plato, *Euthydemus*, in *Complete Works*, 278b-c, p. 715.
7 Kant, *Critique of the Power of Judgment*, p. 206.
8 Ibid.
9 Kant, *Critique of Pure Reason*, p. 110.
10 On dataism and big data, see Han, *Psychopolitik: Neoliberalismus und die neuen Machttechniken*.
11 Heidegger, *Letters to his Wife: 1915–1970*, p. 213
12 Bataille, 'Spiel und Ernst', in Huizinga, *Das Spielelement der Kultur*, p. 111.
13 Baudrillard, *Fatal Strategies*, pp. 187f. [translation modified].

Chapter 10 From Seduction to Porn

1 Baudrillard, *Seduction*, p. 113.
2 Kierkegaard, *The Seducer's Diary*, in *Either/Or: Part I*, p. 318.
3 Foucault, 'The Ethics of the Concern for Self as a Practice of Freedom', in *The Essential Works of Michel Foucault: 1954–1984, Vol. 1*, p. 298.
4 Illouz, *Why Love Hurts*, p. 191.
5 Transl. note: 'Performance' in English in the original.

6 Baudrillard, *Seduction*, pp. 37f.

7 Ibid., p. 38.

8 Transl. note: 'In your face' in English in the original.

9 Transl. note: 'Facial' in English in the original.

10 *Süddeutsche Zeitung*, 27 December 2013.

BIBLIOGRAPHY

Agamben, Giorgio, *Profanations*, New York: Zone Books, 2007.

Agamben, Giorgio, *Nudities*, Stanford: Stanford University Press, 2011.

Agamben, Giorgio and Monica Ferrando, *The Unspeakable Girl: The Myth and Mystery of Kore*, London: Seagull Books, 2014.

Alain, *On Happiness*, New York: Frederick Ungar, 1973.

Arendt, Hannah, *The Human Condition*, Chicago: University of Chicago Press, 1998 [1958].

Badiou, Alain, 'Thinking the Event', in Alain Badiou and Slavoj Žižek, *Philosophy in the Present*, Cambridge: Polity, 2009, pp. 1–48.

Barthes, Roland, *Empire of Signs*, New York: Hill and Wang, 1982.

Barthes, Roland, *The Neutral*, New York: Columbia University Press, 2005.

Basho, Matsuo, *The Complete Haiku*, Tokyo: Kodansha International Ltd., 2008.

Bataille, George, *Die Aufhebung der Ökonomie*, Munich: Matthes & Seitz, 2001.

Bataille, George, 'Spiel und Ernst', in Johan Huizinga, *Das Spielelement der Kultur*, Berlin: Matthes & Seitz, 2014, pp. 75–111.

Baudrillard, Jean, *Seduction*, Montreal: New World Perspectives, 1990.

Baudrillard, Jean, *Von der Verführung*, Munich: Matthes & Seitz, 1992.

Baudrillard, Jean, *Symbolic Exchange and Death*, London: Sage, 1993.

Baudrillard, Jean, *Fatal Strategies*, New York: Semiotext(e), 2008.

Baudrillard, Jean, *The Divine Left: A Chronicle of the Years 1977–1984*, New York: Semiotext(e), 2014.

Baudrillard, Jean, *Das Andere selbst*, Vienna: Passagen, 2016.

Bauman, Zygmunt, *Retrotopia*, Cambridge: Polity, 2017.

Benjamin, Walter, 'The Work of Art in the Age of Its Technological Reproducibility: Second Version', in *The Work of Art in the Age of Its Technological Reproducibility: Second Version and Other Writings*, Cambridge MA: Harvard University Press, 2008, pp. 19–55.

Clausewitz, Carl von, *On War*, New York and London: Alfred A. Knopf, 1993.

Deleuze, Gilles and Félix Guattari, *A Thousand Plateaus*, London: Continuum, 2013.

Douglas, Mary, *Natural Symbols: Explorations in Cosmology*, London and New York: Routledge, 2003 [1970].

Durkheim, Emil, *The Elementary Forms of the Religious Life*, London: George Allen & Unwin Ltd., 1915.

Foucault, Michel, *The Order of Things: An Archaeology of the Human Sciences*, London: Routledge, 1970.

Foucault, Michel, 'Passion According to Werner Schroeter', in *Foucault Live (Collected Interviews 1961–1984)*, New York: Semiotext(e), 1989, pp. 313–21.

Foucault, Michel, 'The Ethics of the Concern for Self as a Practice of Freedom', in *The Essential Works of Michel Foucault: 1954–1984, Vol. 1 (Ethics, Subjectivity and Truth)*, New York: The New Press, 1997, pp. 281–302.

Frazer, James George, *The Golden Bough: A Study in Magic and Religion*, New York: Macmillan, 1925.

Gadamer, Hans-Georg, 'The Relevance of the Beautiful', in *The Relevance of the Beautiful and Other Essays*, trans. Nicholas Walker, Cambridge: Cambridge University Press, 1986.

Garcia, Tristan, *The Life Intense: A Modern Obsession*, Edinburgh: Edinburgh University Press, 2018.

Gennep, Arnold van, *The Rites of Passage*, Chicago: Chicago University Press, 1960.

Han, Byung-Chul, *Hyperkulturalität, Kultur und Globalisierung*, Berlin: Merve, 2005.

Han, Byung-Chul, *Psychopolitik: Neoliberalismus und die neuen Machttechniken*, Frankfurt am Main, 2014.

Han, Byung-Chul, *Topology of Violence*, Cambridge MA: MIT, 2018.

Han, Byung-Chul, *What is Power?*, Cambridge: Polity, 2018.

Handke, Peter, *Phantasien der Wiederholung*, Frankfurt am Main: Suhrkamp, 1983.

Hegel, Georg Wilhelm Friedrich, *Lectures on the Philosophy of History*, London: G. Bell and Sons, 1914.

Hegel, Georg Wilhelm Friedrich, *Aesthetics: Lectures on Fine Art*, Oxford: Clarendon, 1975.

Heidegger, Martin, 'Language in the Poem: A Discussion on Georg Trakl's Poetic Work', in *On the Way to Language*, New York: Harper & Row, 1971.

101

Heidegger, Martin, *Letters to his Wife: 1915–1970*, Cambridge: Polity Press, 2008.

Huizinga, Johan, *Homo Ludens: A Study of the Play-Element in Culture*, London: Routledge & Kegan Paul, 1949.

Illouz, Eva, *Why Love Hurts*, Cambridge: Polity, 2012.

James, William, 'The Gospel of Relaxation', in Robert Richardson (ed.), *The Heart of William James*, Cambridge MA: Harvard University Press, 2010.

Jaspers, Karl, *Philosophie III, Metaphysik*, Berlin and Heidelberg: Springer, 1973.

Kant, Immanuel, *Critique of Pure Reason*, Cambridge: Cambridge University Press, 1998.

Kant, Immanuel, *Critique of the Power of Judgment*, Cambridge: Cambridge University Press, 2002.

Kant, Immanuel, *Anthropology from a Pragmatic Point of View*, Cambridge: Cambridge University Press, 2006.

Kerény, Karl, *Antike Religion*, Stuttgart: Klett-Cotta, 1995.

Kierkegaard, Søren, *The Seducer's Diary*, in *Either/Or: Part I*, Princeton: Princeton University Press, 1987, pp. 301–446.

Kierkegaard, Søren, *Repetition and Philosophical Crumbs*, Oxford: Oxford University Press, 2009.

Kojève, Alexandre, *Introduction to the Reading of Hegel: Lectures on the Phenomenology of Spirit*, Ithaca: Cornell University Press, 1980.

Kojève, Alexandre, *Überlebensformen*, Berlin: Merve, 2007.

Lafargue, Paul, *The Right to Be Lazy*, Chicago: Charles H. Kerr & Company, 1907.

Levinas, Emmanuel, *Totality and Infinity: An Essay on Exteriority*, Dordrecht: Kluwer, 1991.

Marx, Karl, *Die deutsche Ideologie*, MEW, vol. 3, Berlin: Dietz, 1969.

Marx, Karl, 'Economic and Philosophical Manuscripts (1844)', in *Early Writings*, London: Penguin, 1992, pp. 279–400.

Nádas, Péter, *Saját halál*, Pécs: Jelenkor, 2004.

Nádas, Péter, *Behutsame Ortsbestimmung: Zwei Berichte*, Berlin: Berlin Verlag, 2006.

Nádas, Péter, 'A helyzsin óvatos megházozása', in *Hátországi napló: Újabb usszék*, Pécs: Jelenkor, 2006.

Nietzsche, Friedrich, *Beyond Good and Evil*, Cambridge: Cambridge University Press, 2002.

Novalis, *Schriften*, vol. 1, Stuttgart: Kohlhammer, 1960.

Pfaller, Robert, *Das schmutzige Heilige und die reine Vernunft: Symptome der Gegenwartskultur*, Frankfurt am Main: Fischer, 2008.

Pfaller, Robert, *On the Pleasure Principle in Culture: Illusions Without Owners*, London: Verso, 2014.

Plato, *Euthydemus*, in *Complete Works*, Indianapolis: Hackett, 1997.

Plato, *Symposium*, in *Complete Works*, Indianapolis: Hackett, 1997.

Rosa, Hartmut, *Resonances: A Sociology of Our Relationship to the World*, Cambridge: Polity, 2019.

Rosenzweig, Franz, *The Star of Redemption*, Madison: University of Wisconsin Press, 2005.

Saint-Exupéry, Antoine de, *The Wisdom of the Sands*, trans. Stuart Gilbert, New York: Harcourt and Brace & Ward Inc., 1950.

Schmitt, Carl, *The Nomos of the Earth*, New York: Telos Press, 2006.

Sennett, Richard, *The Fall of Public Man*, London: Penguin, 1974.

Sennett, Richard, *Verfall und Ende des öffentlichen Lebens*, Berlin: Berlin Verlag, 2009.

Taubes, Jacob, 'Ästhetisierung der Wahrheit im Posthistoire', in *Apokalypse und Politik: Aufsätze, Kritiken und kleinere Schriften*, Munich: Wilhelm Fink, 2017, pp. 308–17.

Taylor, Charles, *The Ethics of Authenticity*, Cambridge MA: Harvard University Press, 1992.

Türcke, Christoph, *Hyperaktiv! Kritik der Aufmerksamkeitsdefizitkultur*, Munich: C. H. Beck, 2012.